Pursued

An ordinary woman pursued by an extraordinary God

Nikki S. Arnold

www.xulonpress.com

CONTENTS

FORWARD

Fifteen years ago while seeking the Lord's will in prayer, I thought I heard the Lord instruct me to write a book. During my childhood and into adulthood, my father always talked about writing a book. And he did, in fact, write a book. Simon & Schuster conditionally accepted his first novel. Naturally I thought I was hearing my earthly father's voice. I asked Jesus to confirm through one of my friends if it truly was His will. One year passed without confirmation. One morning I had gotten a phone call from my dearest friend Lori Meredith. "Nikki, Jesus woke me up in the middle of the night and said, 'Tell Nikki it is time to write her book.'" Lori laughed and said, "I argued with the Lord and said, 'Lord, Nikki doesn't even keep a journal; how is she going to write a book?'" Jesus repeated His instruction one more time. Lori has been my constant companion in prayer and encouragement over these many years. The stories came bit by bit and now I rest in the knowledge that it has been completed. I accredit Lori's steadfast love and support during the many times I wanted to give up. I also must acknowledge my husband Bill who has become a true hero in encouragement. He stood by me as a valiant prince in protection over his treasured possession. I praise God for His salvation and the healing of our marriage. I want to thank both of my daughters. My oldest daughter, Meagan, edited the first draft of this book with a careful eye. Meg has grown up hearing how the Lord saved her life on the abortionist table. Meagan knows that she is valued and loved with all my heart. I want to thank my daughter Stephanie who has pressed me to persevere to finish. She has been my shining star. To my step-son Christopher and his family thank you for your love. Thank you to all my sisters in Christ for carrying my burden in prayer. I also want to thank my siblings for their love and encouragement. How blessed we all are! Most importantly I thank you Jesus – the one who loved me enough to PURSUE me!

CHAPTER 1
PURSUED

How does an ordinary person give testimony in writing about someone who is extraordinary? With His help, I will try to tell you my story and pray that you will see only Jesus.

The first time I heard His voice, I was just ten years old. I sat in the bathtub with warm water gushing from the spigot's mouth onto a pair of knobby knees. I hated my skinny legs; I was the tallest girl in my class and the boys nicknamed me the class bean pole. Another thing I hated about myself was my blush. Why was I so shy? The kids laughed at me every time the teacher wanted us to speak. My face never failed to become a freckled red tomato when it was my turn to answer the question asked. With a sigh, I dutifully began washing my neck and scrubbing behind each ear.

Suddenly familiar angry voices shouted beyond the bath-room door.

"That's it. I'm not going. You can put your pillow on the couch because that's where you will be sleeping tonight," Mom said.

"Come on, Patty, we haven't been out for a long time. Don't spoil it for the kids," said Dad.

I knew this pattern too well. Dad's been away for a few days and Mom's angry again. I sighed, "Oh please, God, not tonight. I want to go to the drive-in."

An inner male voice said, "Do you want to go through a hard time now or later?"

The voice, quite natural to me as a child, spoke within my personhood; I sat in the tub musing over the question.

I weighed my options and came to the conclusion that we could miss the drive-in movie. "OK. I'll take the hard time now," I said out loud.

Moments later, I was surprised by a pounding on the bathroom door and my father's voice saying, "Hey kiddo – finish up in there. We're going to the movies."

It was funny as I look back on it now. My dad did really want us to go to the drive-in as a family but throughout the whole night I recall only his sharp instruction, "Lie down now. This movie isn't for kids to see."

That was pretty much our life. We had all the upside down and inside out ways of communication like all people had with one another. Silly pranks or games were Dad's interaction with his daughters. Yet, he did train us, infrequently but consistently, with stern lectures on morality and respect for those in authority.

Mom was our steady eddy. She did the hard work of catering to the needs and interests of her girls. The home was her turf. The home itself was clean, kept in order and on schedule. In terms of teaching her four girls manners, care in personal hygiene, providing three meals a day, and nursing us through childhood diseases, my mother was faithful.

Mom's communication to Dad was destructive and demeaning. It was as if she tried to tame a wild bucking horse with the whip of her tongue.

If my mom's way of communicating to her husband was unproductive, my father's way of communication was meaningless. He had complimentary words with empty promises which produced mistrust and disappointment. And when he failed to keep his promises, he ran from those he disappointed for weeks at a time. Dad was the youngest son born to my grandparents who owned a ranch with several acres in western Colorado. Grandpa's first wife died, leaving him with three children that needed care, so that's when he met and married my grandmother who was seventeen years his junior. Grandma's name was Urabelle and she was a Cherokee Indian from Oklahoma. Her picture at a young age showed a strikingly lovely woman with fair skin and large dark eyes. Mom said that my father being the youngest was rather spoiled by his aged father. At the age of seven he drove the family pick-up truck on the ranch and by the age of twelve he had his own checking account — which he over-drew on a regular basis and Grandpa bailed him out without consequences. One of Dad's brother's hung himself once his wife left him because of his alcoholism. The remaining brother gave up his drink and became a religious fanatic.

My mother's history is a bit different. Tragic, really. Mom was just four years old with a younger brother when her father institutionalized her mother at the State Hospital for insanity. He gave away his children to anyone who would take them. Sadly, we heard years later, no one wanted her little brother so he ended up in an orphanage for most of his life. Mom was taken into a home where there was already an infant boy. Unfortunately, once mother joined this little family, her new mother died within two years of breast cancer. Even after Mel, our grandfather, remarried, my mom never felt secure in her new family for she was never legally adopted, and was often referred as a foster daughter all the way into her adult life.

Once mom graduated from high-school, she moved from York to Philadelphia, Pennsylvania, and worked as a payroll clerk in a large supermarket chain. Pictures of a young Patty gave us all an idea why dad found her so attractive. Her long thick black hair curled at its ends and hung beautifully over a tiny delicate frame. They met at a local dance held for the men in the services at the waterfront. Mother was charmed by his vibrant personality and lean handsome figure in a dark naval uniform and white sailor's cap. She was mesmerized by his stories and compliments. He had such big dreams for his future and he asked her to marry him within three short months.

My father and mother had four daughters of average intelligence, appearance, and talent; we had nothing that made any of us stand out among our peers. The Navy had moved us around a lot before basing my Dad in New London, Connecticut. Dad built us a home in a quiet, uneventful small town called Uncasville, and we were surrounded by a group of hardworking people. People much like us — with the usual hopes and dreams.

After twelve years in the Navy, my dad decided to test for the job of 1ST Chief Petty Officer. Since he graduated top of his class in high school, he effortlessly rested upon his natural intelligence without study of the Navy material available. He failed the test and could not face his peers or family. So he disappeared for several weeks until a police officer found my dad – drunk, standing on a large bridge ready to end his life.

My father's nervous breakdown weirdly gave his life and ours a new beginning. He received a large pension with an honorable discharge from the Navy. He and mom decided to use the funds to build a neighborhood Seven Eleven store with a deli shop on its side.

The first couple of years brought great success, and our family earned a reputation of generosity and hard work. Dad's purchases of cars, a home, new furniture, and clothing were proof to himself, and to the world, that he was not a failure.

As the children of the home, we enjoyed the limelight of our family's being in business. For instance, I remember a teacher who asked for donations from our store for a special event at a junior high party. I was as proud as a male peacock when our family's name was publicly acknowledged for the gift.

Two years of working the store, my dad seemingly became bored and made a larger purchase. He bought a nightclub/restaurant in the town of Norwich called the Red Rose Inn. And here it began — the nightmare of an alcoholic's family.

I had a dream when I was 10:

I saw myself cowering in my closet at home, afraid to come out, for I heard there was a murderer in our neighborhood.

Once I found my courage to leave my closet, I entered our friend's house across the street and found only dead people. I ran frantically from house to house, looking for someone, anyone to help me. My heart pounded, sweat dripped down my face, and my hands shook as I witnessed the aftermath of horrible murders of neighbors, their children and even babies in cribs. Where were my parents? Where were my sisters? I decided I must warn the others about the murderer in the neighborhood.

In my dream I suddenly saw myself standing between two policemen. They had caught the murderer and had him handcuffed. I saw his hands with blood on them, and when

I looked up into his face, I was stunned to see that it was my father.

"Dad, why did you do this?" I asked. "I don't understand."

I looked back to the policemen standing and there was my father now dressed in the police uniform.

A voice spoke to me and said, "He will become good again."

Night after night loud arguments between my parents erupted in the wee hours of our mornings. One night, rather, one morning, around 3 a.m., I woke to pleas of my father, "Patty… please let me in. Let me into the house. I need you." His wailings were so loud that it woke all of his children and the neighbors' children. This happened night after night for several months.

During this difficult time my mom and dad sent us to a Congregational church, a little more than a mile's walk from our house. I remember thinking a lot about God. I always wondered about Him. Was He real? Or was He another lie? Like Santa Claus and the Easter Bunny? I joined the children's choir along with my sisters. It was there that I could sense a power around me that I could not see or understand. I was afraid to tell another that I felt this presence of someone watching over me. Mom gave us storybooks of the Old and New Testaments to read; just as she gave us books to read on our bodies when puberty came about. I don't remember her reading any stories with us but she tried her best to answer our questions when asked.

"Mom, how can I be sure that I will go to heaven some day?" I asked.

She wrapped her arm around my shoulders, as we looked out into night from my bedroom window. "You must be good and obey the Ten Commandments."

"What happens if I lie?" I asked. Somehow I surmised that all the commands of God had to be obeyed or I was cast out of heaven for an eternity.

"You need not worry about it until you are twelve," Mom explained. It had something to do with the age of accountability.

Now I pictured God as a God that lived way up high in the heavens with a long white beard, sitting on his white throne with a list of black marks under my name. I knew in my heart I was headed for hell but hoped that God would be kind and overlook all of my faults.

That is how my life went for a number of years until one day, while in junior high school, I came home to an unexpected interruption of my ordinary life.

I stepped off the bus with a promise to call my friend Moira. "Ask your parents about tonight and then call me. I think it'll be okay for me to go to the dance – I just have to make sure," she said. Moira was my newest friend in the 8th grade at Mohegan High School. She had dark brown eyes, a shy smile and was the daughter of a prominent attorney.

My heart lifted thinking about my new friend as I walked home. Finally, I felt as if I fit in with kids in our class at junior high, kids who were like me – shy but not too shy. Kids who wanted to do well but wanted to have fun too.

I walked on the usual path through the woods, cut through the Dugan's backyard, and made my way to the top of Park Ave Ext. where my house sat at the bottom of a hill. As I approached our ranch home, my pulse quickened; I saw a yellow truck parked under the oak tree at our front door.

"Mom? Hey, Mom," I yelled. I made my way through a mish-mash of boxes and a disturbance of furniture throughout our house. My parents both were home and looked fairly happy. "What's going on?" I asked.

"Go sit down in the living room with your sisters and I'll tell you," Dad said.

My sister Jody was already seated on the couch. We were waiting for Kelli to come in from outside, while mom held-three year-old Keitly on her lap. Kelli came bounding in with her dog, Lady, and asked if she could sit on the floor.

"Everybody settled?" asked Mom.

"Girls, in the past we have talked about moving. Today is the day. We're moving this very night to New Mexico. We will be living in a little town called Farmington," Dad said.

"But I wanted to go to the school dance tonight with Moira," I said.

"No. You won't be able to make it," Mom said. "And I don't want you to call her and tell her anything. You'll have to write her a letter once we get there."

Jody started to cry. "Why, New Mexico? It's so far from here and what about the Ukraines? Can't we tell them?"

"Yes, of course, they live across the street. But no one other than our neighbors can know about our move. Do you understand?" Mom asked. "New Mexico is where your grandmother owns a house. That's where we will live."

Dad's eyes looked over our faces. "Hey kids, this is for the best. You'll see. Our family is going to get a fresh start.

You'll make new friends and a whole new world will open up to you."

Kelli's soft hazel eyes looked up into my father's face. "What about Lady? Can Lady come with us?"

"You betcha," my father said.

That was the beginning, certainly, of an unusual life – for all of us.

Our new world started out okay once we crossed the states, climbed the Rocky Mountains and came into the so-called "enchanted land." It was a land quite different from the lush green of New England: a land of square topped mesas, dry brown ground, and dull adobe buildings. A land I wasn't sure I liked at all.

The town at the time consisted of one main street about a mile long with an A&W at its one end and a Frosty Freeze that sat on the other end. I witnessed several Native American men with brown-bagged bottles sprawled along the side of the road. "Who are they, Dad?" I asked. My father explained that they were no good bums and we shouldn't pay any mind to them.

"We are the minority in this town," Dad said. "This area is made up of greasy Mexicans and a whole lot of no-good drunken Indians."

"Nick, please don't speak that way to the girls," Mom scolded.

"It's true. After I graduated from high school, I joined the police force here in Farmington, and I'm telling you we had more problems with Mexicans and gang fights."

"OK. That's enough. You are generalizing. And you're scaring the kids."

"All right, I admit that there are some good, hard-working families that live here or I wouldn't have moved the family to this town, whether we had a house to live in or not."

Grandma's house was a well-laid-out home with five bedrooms and a large fenced yard. It was a safe place for Keitly and Lady the dog. Maybe it will work out here in Farmington, I thought.

My father was hired at the local furniture store. "It'll be just a few months before I'm running that store," announced Dad. I was certain of his claim as well. Dad could do anything, I thought. I knew he thought this job was beneath him yet hopefully he would get where he wanted to be – at the top.

As for the kids, we pretty much adjusted to the schools we were all placed in.

Farmington High School was different yet interesting. I noted the differences between the East and the Southwest, and not only in topography but people. Kids wore cowboy hats and boots to school and talked a lot about rodeos and such.

My first friend, Sue Pitt, often wore a black cowboy hat. Against her fair skin, blonde hair and blue eyes she made a stunning appearance. Not everyone liked Sue, though. She had the reputation of being a spoiled rich kid whose daddy had a ranch house on several hundred acres of land. The others' opinion didn't bother me much. I saw Sue as an outgoing, worldly young girl who loved to have fun. A red-haired, green-eyed Mexican girl named Stephanie, who was on my level of ignorance, was another new friend. Both she and I happened to be star-struck with Sue's friendship and considered her to be the most valued of the three.

One weekend the three of us stayed at the Pitt's ranch house. We were led out far from the house where Sue brought out a pack of cigarettes for us to learn how to smoke.

"Try it like this," said Sue. She took a cigarette between her index and middle finger, lit the cigarette and inhaled. "Here, you do it," she said to Stephanie.

Steph took the cigarette and drew in a breath. "Yuck," she coughed. "Horrible. How can you stand this stuff?"

Sue looked annoyed. "Here, Nikki. You try it," she said.

I took the cigarette but found it too short to smoke. "Do you have another one?" I asked.

She took the butt and threw it down with a stomp of her boot; she pulled out another cigarette from her pack of filtered Camels. "Oh, great - no more matches. Let's go back to the ranch and I'll get another pack."

We walked on a dirt path through two large wild bushes that bordered opposite sides of a plank. We scurried across the creek below, meeting open land ahead of us. The whole way Sue talked about her new boyfriend, Patrick. "He's Mexican. My family would have a fit, so let's keep it quiet. Patrick loves me and he loves what I have to give him." Stephanie shot a quick look at me. I said nothing.

I was the last to leave the bushes and cross the plank. As soon as I hopped off the plank, a man appeared from the bushes on the other side.

"Hey girls," a dirty face with unshaved stubble poked through the bush. "I couldn't help but hear that you are in need of matches. If you want them, I've got a pack." His large hand opened and motioned for us to come.

Sue started to walk slowly toward the man. "Er, thanks."

An uneasy feeling swelled in my stomach and I suddenly heard a male voice within my heart say, "Run. NOW - run." I ran up to Sue, grabbed her by the elbow and screamed, "Run!"

Stephanie, Sue and I screamed all the way to the Pitt's ranch. Mrs. Pitt called the police and had a patrolman come out to check the entire area. Nothing was found but a pack of matches and a few cigarette butts scattered about.

The next morning, the front page of the Farmington News read, *Three Convicts from Colorado State Prison Captured!* Unfortunately, it was that very evening the men entered a shoe store where there had been a lone woman clerk. They raped, robbed and stabbed her twice in the back. The men left her for dead until another customer entered the shop and called the police. The authorities found the prisoners hiding two miles into the desert. They couldn't go far because of the chains around their ankles.

The three of us girls were shaken to the core about this experience. I thought about the voice that saved our lives. What or who was that? The one thing I knew for sure was that there was nothing ordinary about my life.

And if it wasn't then that I knew my life was not ordinary, it was certainly when Dad made headlines in that very paper just weeks later.

CHAPTER 2
DESERTION

D ad's expectations of becoming the furniture store's manager/owner hadn't materialized. This time he left us for three months. We all felt his absence for he was never gone this long before.

"Where is Daddy?" asked Keitly.

Mom pulled Keitly up on her lap and combed her fingers through a mop of blonde hair. Jody walked up to Mom, leaned on her arm, and asked, "When is Dad coming back?" She sat down at Mom's side with inquisitive large brown eyes.

"He'll be back," I said. "He always comes back."

"Why did he go in the first place?" Kelli asked. "Is he mad at us?"

"Phew, Kel. Go take a bath. All I can smell is Lady," I said. Kelli's right hand picked a brown strand of hair and placed it behind her ear.

"Leave Kelli alone, Nikki," Jody said standing up with her chest out. "You're not her boss."

"Girls - stop bickering! Dad will be back when he works through his problems. For right now, I'm going to have to find a job."

We kids suddenly grew quiet. "Mom, I'm scared. Are we going to be okay?" Jody asked.

My mother stood up with a smile on her face. "Of course we're going to be okay." Mom's re-assurance wasn't all that convincing but the younger sisters accepted it without question.

One day after school ended, my mother met me at the door with a newspaper in her hand. "Look what your father has done!" I looked up into my mom's swollen eyes.

My stomach flip-flopped. With racing heartbeats I took the newspaper from her hand. The front-page headline was: *"National Manhunt for Farmington's Ex-Policeman."* I staggered back and asked, "What does this mean?"

"He's wanted for manslaughter in Massachusetts. He robbed an elderly man who kept nine thousand dollars in his house, probably under his mattress The old man died of a heart attack while being robbed," she cried. "Your dad's fingerprints were all over the rope around the body."

Stunned and shaken I tried to take it all in. My father robbed someone? The man died? How? Why? This has to be a mistake! "Dad wouldn't do something like this," I said.

"Tell that to those who are looking for him. There were two FBI agents here this morning. Your father is nowhere to be found. The agents thought I might be hiding him," Mom said.

I ran to the bathroom and heaved over the toilet. My dad killed someone? He was a criminal? I listened to the wails of my sisters in the next room. Pain seared my heart. I stood alone in the bathroom unable to move, unable to comprehend.

The sharp sword of devastation pierced our household. We didn't know what to do with this information. We felt the shame and desertion among our neighbors and peers. My friends Susie and Stephanie didn't know what to do with my pain. I was no longer included or invited to join them in any of our school functions. I became the prey of the jealous or the insecure. Now I was their target of ridicule.

Sandra was a girl who befriended me the first week I moved to New Mexico. My parents forbid our friendship because they felt that Sandra dressed scantily and had too many boyfriends. I knew she was hurt, and expected me to stand up against my parents, but I would not. There was a day at school, where our paths met, and Sandra took her revenge. Sandra stopped me on my way to class and said, "So your dad is too good for me? He's gotta a lot of nerve." Sandra, being much bigger than I, threw me down onto the ground with a wad of my hair in her left hand while her fisted right hand punched me in the face. A teacher interrupted the beating by pulling her off of me and taking Sandra down to the principal's office.

As I look back, I can see that my beating from Sandra created concern from a high school counselor. Two junior girls named Kim and Sherry befriended me, apparently at the request of the counselor. The girls made their introduction, and offered to pick me up for school. Kim and Sherry also invited me to spend Friday nights with them, and in general accepted me into their fellowship. At the time, I could not figure out why these two long-legged beauties would want to hang out with me. But they did. They never pressed me for information about my dad or asked to come into my home. One night they asked me if I wanted to go to church with them. "Sure. I'll go," I said.

We walked in and sat on the last pew nearest the door. Sherry's blonde hair had been pulled back into a ponytail.

She wore black and white checked pants with a red shirt. Kim wore a long blue skirt that hung down below her knees with a matching headband that kept dark bangs out of her large gray eyes. "We grew up in this church," Kim whispered. "This is where Sherry and I met when we were five years old."

The church was packed. I was glad to be sitting in the back. I didn't want anyone to notice me. The preacher was as loud as any human could be. After an opening prayer, the minister went into his sermon with loud shouts of damnation. "You people are going to go to hell if you don't believe in Jesus. Hell is full of fire and brimstone with millions of souls gnashing their teeth in deep regret. The devil is looking for you to join them." He ranted on and on until I was most uncomfortable. I looked over at my two friends and they were weeping. The preacher said, "Anyone who wants God to save you from damnation, come up here – now."

I froze. I looked over at Sherry who had dropped to her knees in the aisle. Kim joined her friend, and they crawled side by side on their hands and knees to lay prostate before the preacher.

I watched and waited for his prayer to be finished. I squirmed in my seat as I looked for an easy exit. Although I wanted to run out of there, I decided to wait until the preacher was done with my friends. After the service my new friends' faces glowed as they returned back to the pew.

Once we left the building, Kim asked, "What did you think about our church?"

"Scary," I said honestly. The girls looked at one another and giggled. "Yeah, I guess it can be a little scary," said Sherry.

That night we spent the night at Sherry's house. The girls told me the reason for our trip to the church that evening: "We played with the Ouija Board a few days ago."

"What's that?" I asked.

"I'll show you," Sherry said. She went into her closet and pulled out a game that said "Ouija." "See the alphabet and numbers. If you ask the board a question while resting your fingers on this white triangle with another person it spells out the answers."

Kim said, "Sherry, get rid of it. I don't want to play with it again."

"Oh believe me, I don't either. I just wanted to show it to Nikki."

They both acted scared. "Why are you afraid?" I asked.

The girls said in unison, "Because the devil talks through it."

"What? Are you kidding?" I asked.

Then they told me their story. "Last week we played with it and asked it questions like when are we going to die? And you know what it said?"

I shook my head.

"It said 1971. That's next year," Kim said. "And what was really scary, the board kept spelling out that it hated me but loved Sherry."

"Oh come on," I said.

"No really. The next night we went up to the mesa for a bonfire with some friends. Not one person knew that the two of us played with the board. After the party, we went back to our car where somebody had written on the dusty windshield – I love Sherry; I hate Kim."

A rush of fear washed over me. "There had to be someone there who knew about the game," I said.

"No, Nikki. No one knew," Sherry said. Kim started crying. "Throw it away Sherry. Throw that game away."

That night was a night of bonding. True friendship developed as I could see my friends were genuine and shared their thoughts and fears with me.

At home the bills were piling up and Mom couldn't find a full time job. Christmas came and went without one gift given among our family. With the threat of our electricity being shut off, Mother began selling the furniture. "We have to have lights and food to eat," she said.

My grandfather, Mom's dad, had offered his help. He bought five airplane tickets to move us out, with only the clothes on our backs, to Pennsylvania. It was tough saying goodbye to Sherry and Kim. My friends and their parents asked me to stay with them until the school year was finished. And that was something I really wanted to do, but my mother would not give her consent.

"No, Nikki. You're part of this family. Remember blood is thicker than water. These girls are good friends but your family is more important," Mom said. My friends were disappointed but promised to write me each week once we were settled.

I looked out the window as the plane descended for landing. The green rolling hills, a river that swayed to the left and right bordered by trees of brilliant colors of orange, yellow and red greeted our arrival.

My grandparents met us with two cars for our travel to the new home that was purchased for Mom and her girls. I warily watched my grandfather's interaction with Mom. Mel was a stiff board with little emotion. His spectacles rested on his long pointed nose as he drove and spoke in a low quiet voice. "He's a no good bum. Always has been. We warned you about him."

"Thank you, Dad, for helping us. I will pay you back as soon as I can get back on my feet."

"I've arranged the payment plan with the bank I use. Once you get a job, we'll talk about the amount, interest, and length of the loan," said Mel.

We were driven for what seemed to be hours out into the countryside of York County. I watched the farmlands, and empty meadows pass by and started to cry.

"What's wrong, Nikki?" Mom asked.

"We're so far away from anything – there's nothing around here. Do we have to live way out here?"

Grandpa raised his eyebrows at my words. "Young lady, this trailer park is the only one I could find that took four kids. Be thankful that I found this place, or where would you all be now?"

I hated the trailer park. It consisted of nine trailers positioned of both sides on one street. The woods that surrounded the park gave it an eerie, lonely feeling. Chester, the park owner, showed us to our new home, a fully furnished, three bedroom, new trailer.

I watched Chester, who was grossly overweight with rotted teeth and greasy hair, instruct the rules of trailer park life and lot rental to my mother. "I expect payment on the first of each month. No loud parties or family fights. If you stick to our rules you'll find no problem with me."

The people in the trailer park were much like Chester. Shirtless toddlers played in their yards, even though it was the season of fall. Later we met the mothers of these babies who had no interest in cleanliness for their children or their homes. They did have an interest in teen girls to babysit their children as they bar-hopped on the weekends. I refused to babysit after I witnessed the infestation of fleas in one dirty trailer. The three little ones that I had charge over had open sores from infected flea bites. A mangy dog remained in the home, and I refused to ever go back in.

"Dear Kim and Sherry," I wrote. "I'm surrounded by hicks- rednecks they call themselves. There's a town at the bottom of a hill where our trailer park sits called 'Bittersville.' Can you believe it? The town has a small church, a corner grocery store, and a few houses on one street. There is a gang of bad guys who ride on motorcycles; they call themselves the Dirt Hogs, and they live there. I don't think I'll be spending much time in that little town."

"You wouldn't believe this school we now attend. It has no football games. They have only basketball. And the kids are mean. They step on the heels of our shoes as we walk in the halls to our next class. Every day I wish that I could be somewhere else."

Another week I wrote: "I ended up having a knock-down, drag-out fight with someone on our bus. She was giving Kelli a hard time. I'm sick of it."

Kim and Sherry together would write their letters faithfully every week. They tried to cheer me up with a thought that we would someday re-unite whether it was after graduation or a visit in the summer months.

After a few months, I suddenly didn't receive my weekly letters. "Do you think my friends are tired of writing to me?" I asked my mother. "It hasn't even been a year."

After two or three weeks, I received a letter from a friend of my sister Jody. "Why is Lou writing me?" I asked out loud. I opened the letter and a newspaper clipping fell out:

Two Teenage Girls Die: Head On Collision

I screamed and fell down into a ball. "What is this? No, God, no, please not them." Jody ran over to me and asked, "What happened?" I held out the newspaper article with Kim's and Sherry's faces on it. She fell to my side, held me and said, "It reads that they were driving too fast on a wet road and hit a truck head on. They were both decapitated."

"Jody, I can't take much more. How much more can we all take?"

I remembered Kim and Sherry's experience from the Ouija board. The accident was at the year's end of 1971 – the same year the Ouija Board predicted.

CHAPTER 3
A ROOT OF BITTERSVILLE

Trailer life in Bittersville, Pennsylvania, was exactly as you would imagine for outsiders.

We girls were mocked, ridiculed, stepped on, and slandered for the first year. Acne wracked my face, and constipation attacked my bowels. My mother's low-paying K-Mart job brought new responsibilities for the four of us to care for our home. The cloud of poverty, the knowledge of my father's imprisonment and my parents' divorce weighed heavily upon me.

Our family no longer appeared as a unit. We weren't the same anymore. Hormones and temperaments were out of whack. I resented being put in the position of adulthood. I hated that I had to work. I hated when mom began dating. I hated that I had to share a bed. I hated my grandfather for placing the trailer in Bittersville. But I did make friends in school and spent the majority of my time away from home.

My mom found that while I was gone - it was better. She gave up the fight and asked me to leave our home for good when I was in my senior year. We fought constantly about work or school. The changes in my life were too enormous for me to handle.

I sought be a so-called good girl and was known to be the last virgin in the class. That changed when I fell in love with a boy two years older than myself. He was a handsome athlete who loved life, music and tennis. He was the ultimate of cool at the time. The young man was with me when my mother was not. He stood by me throughout the last year of high school while I was living at my friend's home. He encouraged me as I worked at a local factory to pay rent. He asked me to marry him after my high graduation. At my graduation, he was the only one who attended.

I did it because I felt I had nowhere else to go. My options were limited. I could work in a sewing factory to earn a higher income than say a cashier at Kmart - or marry someone who would take care of me. He had a good job as a land surveyor and a promise of a bright future. I opted for the easy road.

I was eighteen years old when we married and moved to the Pocono Mountains. We were both immature. I was filled with insecurity, inferiority, and total dependency upon him. He was self-centered with his own inferiority complex that would turn into rage when challenged. I knew he had a temper before I had married him, but never considered that his temper would get out of hand within days of our marriage. He threw me down a flight of stairs the first week we were married because I fussed at him for being three hours late from work. That was the beginning of a four-month nightmare. On more than one occasion he beat me so hard my ears bled. The beatings I received were humiliating and degrading and at times very public.

After a beating in the local mall, we got into his little red VW Bug to go home. My sobs penetrated the silence in our car. I could feel his regret but had no desire to allow him to speak. He decided to stop for something to eat and asked if I wanted anything. "No, no, nothing," I said.

He got out of the car, and I saw that he left the keys in the ignition and his cash envelop of his weekly pay. I locked my door and then climbed over to the driver's seat and locked his door. I turned the key in the ignition and bucked out of the parking lot. He had been teaching me how to drive stick, but I had never had the car alone before. I raced the little car home, threw my clothes in a suitcase and ran out of our home shaking from head to toe. "God, please. Get me out of here."

The ride back to York County was nearly three hours and I prayed the entire way through the mountains, truck traffic, and rain. My heart was sick but I was determined to leave him and never go back. I needed refuge and I had no place to go.

I hoped that my sister Jody would allow me into her home. She had married to get out of the house less than two years ago, at the age of 17. Jody was a homecoming princess, straight A student and now a parent of a little boy. Jody did offer me refuge while she herself was experiencing abuse within her marriage. Jody's marriage soon ended and we were both divorcees before the age of twenty.

CHAPTER 4
DOWNWARD SPIRAL

I had another dream:

I saw myself driving on a long stretch of road by the Susquehanna River. It was a beautiful day and I was conscious of the fact that I had much to do. Surprisingly, I saw my father standing at the side of the road. I stopped and asked, "Do you need a ride?" He smiled at me with his lopsided grin, pulled out a gun from his jacket and shot me in the neck. My foot pressed onto the gas pedal, and I sped away with blood and confusion. I knew I had been critically wounded but kept pressing onto a winding road that brought me through small and large towns alike. Whenever I saw a human being, I asked for directions to the hospital, but no one could show me the way.

This nightmare foreshadowed eight years of a winding road looking for help in love relationships, jobs, travel, and education. I found nothing but emptiness, rejection, failure, rage, and thoughts of ending my life. I did have intermittent moments of successes in love, friendships, job accomplishments, and the birth of my daughter, Meagan.

At the start of my 8-year nightmare, my Father was released early from prison. He tested well for an educational program at the University of Massachusetts as part of the government's efforts to reform criminals by providing opportunities for a higher education. He had turned into an intellectual hippie while serving time in prison. It was at the University that my father met Eileen and also began smoking marijuana. Wanting and needing his attention, I accepted his invitation to travel to the Virgin Islands, and Cape Cod, Massachusetts, with him. "I want to show you girls that there is a whole different world out there," he said. "You are young and beautiful and need to experience more of life than you have until this point."

My father was shocked and angry that Jody and I had married so young, and that Kelli was about to marry. "Please come with us for awhile," he begged. We understood that our relationship with him now included a new person – Eileen. Eileen was nice, but we didn't understand why she had left her four young children to travel with Dad.

Jody, Kelli and I joined them in the Virgin Islands for a summer while he worked as an overseer/manager of apartments on the beach. In fact, Kelli left for the Islands in the nick of time before she too had married.

When I arrived in San Croix, I felt as if I had arrived in paradise. The Caribbean clear water, palm trees, and white sands were incredibly beautiful. Yet there was hatred in the air. I feared walking alone on the island, as whites were not welcome by the Islanders during off-tourist season.

"Why do these men hiss at us?" I asked.

"They're just ignorant," Eileen said. "Don't you remember reading in the papers a couple of years ago about the white golfers killed on the golf course? They were killed because they were white."

"Great," I said. "That makes me feel real good about living here."

"Just don't pay any attention to them. Don't look at them in their eyes. Keep your head down," Dad said.

I enjoyed my father's personality, craved his fellowship, but soon understood that he had changed. And it wasn't for the better. My dad who was an incurable romantic happened to be an alcoholic and now a pot smoker. Eileen was more than just a smoker. She had pretended to be pregnant when she traveled on the airline as she visited her kids in Boston and returned to San Croix. She brought with her, under her pregnancy shirt, several pounds of marijuana.

"Are you crazy? What if you get caught?" I asked.

Eileen laughed and said, "I suppose there's that possibility, but it's unlikely that anyone would consider me to be a dealer." An uneasy feeling grew in my belly. What were we in the middle of?

Eileen and Dad fought a lot. She wanted her children with her as he had his with them. Dad didn't want the younger kids living with us. He said it was too difficult to live on this island as it was without worrying about little ones.

I suppose he referred to the recent break-ins of the apartments he managed. There was a peeper who nearly raped a white woman who lived alone. Somehow she was able to get away and others captured the boy. He was an Islander about 17 years old. Dad called the cops and tied the kid to a palm tree until the police made their way over, which took several hours. The boy was pistol whipped and threatened by some of the residents.

"Dad, let the kid go," I pleaded.

"Not yet, he's going to learn a lesson. See the cops are corrupt here. Everyone is a relative and they shut their eyes to crime. So let the people take care of him," Dad said.

It was about that time that Eileen finally left for good. She couldn't live away from her children any longer.

Dad was miserable and was drinking more heavily. He'd disappear for days at a time and show up only when it was necessary. When several weeks passed, I went out looking for Dad and I found him sitting out on the side of the road - drunk. The smell of whiskey nauseated me.

"I hate that woman, she makes my life miserable," he slurred his words at me. "Tell me, Nikki, why do I want her back?"

"Dad, let's move back to the States," I suggested. "That way you can try to work things out with Eileen." My suggestion was selfish. I never really felt comfortable on the Island as my two sisters did. Jody and Kelli had legitimate lives on the Island. They loved the waters, felt at home with the Islanders and had a hard time leaving, but they did agree that we should all be together in the states.

So, we moved to Cape Cod. We rented a cottage from a friend of my dad's, and things seemed okay for a while. Jody and I got jobs at the local supermarket, and Kelli worked at a Burger King. And we rotated in caring for Jody's little boy, Jason.

It was a time of tension and regret. I felt sick about this situation, moving around with Dad. We really didn't have a clue how to take care of ourselves, yet we knew we had to learn fast. I couldn't go back to Mom's house, even though the two of us resolved our differences during my divorce. My mother still had Keitly at home and married the man she was dating. Plus he had children of his own with child support responsibilities.

Dad's habits were pulling us all down. I felt we were all drowning because of his inability to stay away from the bottle.

We lived in a small white Cape house with a few pieces of mismatched beach furniture with a small sandy yard gated by a worn-out red wooden fence. I wanted to be rescued; our dad was not at all what we as his children remembered him to be. We became aware of the fact that dad was not our rescuer when we noticed money missing.

"Dad, don't you think we know that you forged Kelli's name on the back of her paycheck?" Jody said. "That's really low. How could you do that?"

"I guess that's what you do when you don't want to work," Kelli replied.

"Maybe its best you go live with Eileen in Boston," I suggested.

Dad left. We worked and lived on our own on the Cape. Everything we did was humdrum, until I met a man named Wayne.

CHAPTER 5
HEARTBREAK AVENUE

"I'll go into the restaurant and get change for five dollars," I said. Our weekly call home to Mom usually was on a Saturday afternoon from a pay phone. I opened the wood door of The Mooring and looked past the few people at round tables. There stood a young man behind the bar. He had a mop of curly hair with a wide grin of straight, white teeth.

"No problem. How much change did you want? You're not from around here are you?" he asked.

"No. I just spent a few months on San Croix. My family is from Pennsylvania," I said.

"Welcome to the Cape. Our season is over; so you might think the town is a little boring, but we're glad for the break."

With change in hand I walked toward the door. "Hey, my name is Wayne. My brother and I own this place. If you ever need anything, I might be able to help in some way."

"Thanks. My name is Nikki."

I walked out of the building over to the telephone booth. "There's a cute guy in there. Anytime we need change, I volunteer."

I didn't think too much more about Wayne until a week or so later when Jody and I decided to go to lunch at Burger King to see Kelli. As we walked with Jason in his stroller on Main Street, a brown LTD pulled up alongside of us. "Do you girls need a ride?" he asked.

It was the fellow from behind the bar. "Hey, that's him - the guy who gave me change for the phone booth," I whispered to Jody.

"No, thank you. We are going to have lunch over at the Burger King," I said.

"May I join you?" he asked. "I'll buy!"

"Sure," Jody said. As he pulled away, Jody giggled.

"I think he has a crush on you, Nikki."

Wayne walked into the restaurant with khaki pants, a blue sweater with a popped collar reaching to a mop of brown curls. He joined Jody and me for a cheeseburger and fries. "Are you sisters enjoying the Cape?"

"It's okay. It's a little hard to get to know people around here," Jody said.

I listened as he spoke about the people on the Cape and talked about the seasonal tourism or those that have made their home in Hyannis. "People are people. In the summer we are into everyone's business but by winter we hibernate. Hey, did you get to see the Kennedy's Compound?"

"You can't see much of it because of the high fence," I said. "But yes, we saw it."

After some more small talk, it was time to leave. Wayne cast his eyes downward and hesitated before he said, "I have to confess, I've been trying to find you ever since you walked into my restaurant. I hope you don't mind."

"I told you, Nikki," Jody said.

This time it was my turn to blush. I was speechless.

All I remember were his large green eyes and his shy grin. Over dinner the next evening, I found out more about this man. He was eight years older than I, had purchased his own home, and wanted to establish his own restaurant. He told me about his service in the Vietnam War as a helicopter pilot. He still loved to fly in the National Guard. He shared his home with another brother.

I was swept away in a whirlwind romance. Wayne was kind, considerate, and romantic. One day, months into our relationship, I came home from work and found a decorated Christmas tree with a beautiful new winter coat packaged under it. Wayne's thoughtful pursuit was incredibly romantic.

Still, our relationship was unevenly matched. I had unreasonable rage with an inferiority complex. He was self-confident, sarcastic, and cold at times. He rarely drank, and I drank all the time. He had it all together and I had nothing together. Nearly two years into our relationship, I was pregnant.

One afternoon, I sat with Dee, a mutual friend of ours, for lunch at the restaurant. Often, the three of us went to the theatre or had dinner together. Dee was a girl I loved because of her quick-wit and cheerful personality except at times where she became sullen and moody, usually around Wayne.

Dee pushed her plate away, and took a large sip of her iced tea. "You can't marry Wayne," she said. I watched her blue eyes burn red with tears.

"Why?" I asked. A strange lump rose up into my throat. "I'm pregnant - I have to marry Wayne."

"I love him," she said. "I don't know what I'll do if you two marry. I'm a good girl, Nikki. I gave myself to him before you came into his life."

I was stunned. How many times had I asked him about their friendship before me? Did I not sense this, and yet Wayne said it was all in my head. I was enraged. How could he make such a fool out of me? And now I was having a child with him?

After confronting Wayne, I left the Cape. I went to stay with my dad and Eileen in Brookline, a suburb of Boston, for a few weeks.

I was made to feel welcome in the house that Dad and Eileen rented with her four children. Jody came to stay, too, for a while before she joined Kelli back on the island. Dad and Eileen seemed to be good. He was painting houses for a living, and she was working as a secretary in a reading facility.

I cried. I waited. I cried, and waited for Wayne to come after me.

"Nikki, I'm not going to tell you what to do but if I were you, I would get an abortion," Dad said. "You're a woman who has the world by its tail. The last thing you need to do is have a baby on your own."

Wayne finally did call me, but it wasn't to ask me to for-give him. He asked me to get an abortion. "Nikki, it's not going to work. I'll send you the money for the abortion. If you want me to go with you, I will."

"No thanks. Just send the money." I was furious and broken. My heart was seared in two. If a heart could bleed, mine was gorging out pints of blood. In my mind's eye, I saw myself with a shotgun. I entered Wayne's restaurant, raised the gun, aimed and fired.

I scheduled an appointment for an abortion. With past pregnancy scares, I would pray, "Please, God, let me get my period. Please this one time. I'm not ready to have a baby. If I do get pregnant, I won't get an abortion." But here I was at the abortionist.

The cold clinical room had several young women sit-ting in the waiting room. This was my second visit. The first is for confirmation of your pregnancy and determination of how many weeks the fetus is in your womb. The second visit is for the abortion itself. The young girls in the waiting room sat in gloomy silence.

I thought of my life. I needed to get my life together. Living these few weeks at my dad's was driving me crazy. Drug trafficking was their 'extra money' to meet the bills;

made me fear arrest. Plus, Eileen wasn't a housekeeper and cared nothing about cleanliness. It drove me crazy. I had to get out. My father's household brimmed over with any and all things I knew I didn't want. I had applied for an apartment, had a job and a roommate named, Karen. And now I had plans to establish my life without Wayne and without a baby.

Suddenly, my name was called.

CHAPTER 6
INTERRUPTION

It was my turn. I rose up from my seat and walked slowly into the room for my abortion.

"Here, change into this," said a dark haired nurse. "And then lie on the table with your feet into the stirrups. The doctors will be here shortly." I searched her face and saw nothing. The nurse showed no compassion, nor interest, only a look of distain.

"Why two doctors?" I asked.

"One's an anesthesiologist. You do want to be anesthetized?" she asked. A stainless steel tray was held in her left hand while she shuffled through the small vials on the counter with her right.

Yes. I wanted anything that would prevent pain. With my nod, the nurse left me without a word. Mechanically, I took off my clothes and put on the clinic's sterile green robe. The table was narrow and long with a clean white paper draped down its middle. I obediently climbed upon the table and placed both heels onto the cold metal stirrups.

Suddenly a male voice spoke within my heart, "You promised God you would not do this. Are you going to break your promise?"

I squirmed. I remembered.

"Are you going to break your promise to GOD?"

My chest sank as if someone was sitting on it. I looked up to see the two physicians. One doctor stood at my right arm preparing a syringe. The other doctor stood somewhere at my feet.

The voice spoke again "To GOD?"

Sweat beads dripped down my face as my whole body shook. I couldn't break my promise to God. What kind of trouble would I reap? I cried out, "No! No, I can't break my promise to God."

Both physicians left the room to my great surprise. I lay there in silence while looking up at the ceiling when the nurse returned. "Get up and get dressed," she said curtly. "The receptionist will return your money."

Once I stood up and dressed I felt as if there were a ton of bricks lifted off of my chest, and, strangely I felt peace.

I rode the trolley back to my dad's house and wondered, "Now what?"

I walked into my father's home and told them what I didn't do. Eileen burst into tears and said, "Oh, thank God."

I looked at her with confusion. "I thought you wanted me to have an abortion."

"Never! I was told to stay out of it, but I can tell you I was praying that you would not do such a thing," said Eileen.

Then, I had another Dream:

I was standing in front of a large white house with two pillars. My father and his wife were slumped up against the front door of the house, and both had wine bottles in their hands. I tried to talk to them yet they weren't making sense because of their inebriation. In the meantime, a huge lion's arm came from the window of the right side of the house. The lion's paw took a swipe at me. I ran to the other side of the house, the left arm of the lion reached out of the window to claw at me. I couldn't get away from the house no matter how hard I tried.

For months I wrestled with that dream and knew that it had significance. I wondered about its meaning often. It wasn't until I moved out into my own apartment with my friend Karen that I received an unusual phone call. I was home alone, messing in my kitchen when the phone rang.

"Hello. I'm calling from a dream center in Boston," he said. "I was wondering if I could interpret a dream for you?" The man's kind voice intrigued me. I willingly and immediately shared my dream with him.

"You poor child," he said. "You've had a very difficult decision to make. And it had to be made. It wasn't something you could walk away from. The two arms of the lion represent two strong forces vying for your decision. I am sure you made the right decision."

CHAPTER 7
A VISIT

"You need to sign up for welfare, Nikki," said Eileen. "That's the only way you will be able to cover doctor bills and the hospital."

"I guess you're right. But Karen got me another job at Boston University. They pay $25 an hour to model for the art students. The professor wants me to come into his class three times a week, for an hour each time. I have to get rid of the furniture sales job. My boss is a pig."

"Keep the modeling job. Don't tell the Welfare Department anything about that. You could use the extra money," she said.

Karen and I originally thought Jody and/or Kelli would join us by sharing our nice new apartment, but they opted to go back to the Islands for a season or two. Karen was a great help and friend. She was a student at University of

Massachusetts and worked as a waitress at a restaurant in Faneuil Hall.

During my pregnancy, I read every book on natural child-birth that I could get my hands on. I hired a mid-wife and decided to have my baby at home. Wayne had been calling and had agreed to pay for all that I needed. I still ached and resented his obvious rejection. He had another girlfriend by the time I was eight months pregnant. I burned with anger. Wayne asked me if he could be present at the birth of our child. At first I agreed.

On December 20 at 12:00 a.m. my labor began. About three in the morning, flakes of snow showered down upon my head as I silently walked the city block. Karen walked with me as we strode noiselessly in the morning hour. After an hour or so, Karen grew weary so, once my mid-wife came and calls to Dad and Eileen were made, she went to bed. By that time I was in the full swing of hard labor. I clung to the shower rod, naked and wet. "Oh, God, help me," I cried. I made my way back to my room, dressed in my nightgown and crawled onto my bed where the mid-wife checked my cervix.

"You're not moving past two centimeters and it's nearly eighteen hours," she said with a wrinkled brow.

I heard my father pace my living room floor. "Nikki, let's go to the hospital," he cried. The hushed whispers of the mid-wife and family heightened while I labored on.

"I think it's time to go to the hospital, you may need a Caesarian," the mid-wife said.

My father and Eileen escorted me to their car. It was the wildest drive I had ever experienced. My father's hands were shaking as his foot slammed onto the gas pedal. "Nick, please. You're going to kill us," Eileen said. We arrived safely at the emergency room of the Beth Israel Hospital.

During four more hours of labor, Eileen coaxed me to pant and breathe between contractions. She stood by my side with kindness, compassion, and steadfast confidence. "You're almost there, Nikki. You can do it," she said.

At one point, I saw a flicker of concern in her eyes when I said, "I'm not going to make it. I guess this is how I'm going to die." I thought about the many rules I had broken over the years and had fear in meeting God.

It was at 1:05 a.m. on the 21st of December, I birthed a seven-pound, six ounce, beautiful little girl with light hair and rosy cheeks. She had been in a posterior position, which made it extremely difficult to deliver. I marveled at her perfection and wondered how anyone could deny that there is a God once they witnessed the birth of a child?

I wrestled in thought about Wayne. I refused to call him during labor when I knew he wanted to be there. And I delighted in his tears when he was finally called a couple of days later. "He can cry on his new girlfriend's shoulder," I said. My revenge was sweet for an instant, but I wrestled with guilt for a long time.

As a new, single mommy, I felt overwhelmed and inadequate to say the least. I never really babysat, maybe a little, so everything was new to me. I got out my books, and connected with a pediatrician for my little girl. Karen was a help yet she had enough on her shoulders with school work, a job and a boyfriend.

I did meet with Wayne one day. I looked at him and felt sorry for him. "Wayne, if you want to be a daddy to Megs and help me raise her that's fine. I want you to do so. But you have to promise me that you will always be there for her, never turn away from her or drop her out of your life once you get married and have other children. If you can't promise me that, then leave us alone."

That evening Wayne promised me and over the years has kept to his word. I kept to my word that I would never keep her from him and I would not raise the child support payment that we agreed upon.

GAZING

Gazing through a pane of glass
Wondering how long
Will this new predicament last
Bored with a literary jaunt
My reflection, a shadowed gaunt
Tired of
Murky dark thoughts of shame
LORD, it was then you called me by name

One night, Meagan who was but a few weeks old, lay sleeping in her cradle next to my bed. It was 11:00 p.m., and I was in the middle of reading one of the latest books my father had lent me. Dad encouraged me to read classics, novels, poetry and non-fiction. He wanted me to experience every kind of good writer. This particular book was Henry Miller's book titled, *The Tropic of Capricorn*. I grew bored with it and stared out my bedroom window at the back brick building that stood three floors taller than our building. The building was empty. I was empty. I stared out at the blank windows and thought of my life. I was scared. What was I going to do?

I made a decision in my heart. "I'm going to be the best mother that I can be," I said out loud. "I'll go back to school and work to support my own child. I don't need to be married to Wayne or anybody else."

Suddenly, a voice spoke into my ear - a male voice - and this time he softly said, "Nikki." I froze. My room filled with a strong electrifying presence and my first thought was: is this God? My second thought was: right, God would enter my room just to see me. Am I going crazy? It is true I have had a difficult time this last year. Maybe I am having a breakdown. I decided to turn my light off and go to sleep.

Once I turned off my light, the presence intensified. I quickly turned the light back on. I didn't want to remain in the dark with whatever was happening. My heart had been beating quite fast. I tried again to ignore the presence; so I picked up my book to read. The first words my eyes read were: "The Meek Shall Inherit the Earth."

I sat up in my bed for another hour or so until the presence went away. The next morning, I got up and called the Mental Health Center in Brookline Village. I was given an appointment immediately. I left Meg with Karen and walked to the center.

There was a Jewish man with round-rimmed glasses who sat behind a desk. He offered me a seat. I quietly but shyly gave him every part of what had happened to me the night before. "Do you think that I am losing my mind? I have had such a hard time of it this past year."

He stared at me for a few moments before he said, "How do you know that it wasn't God?"

I left the Center with more questions. Why me?

CHAPTER 8
THE CHASE

O ver the next few years I ran. I ran away from God as far and fast as I could go. I didn't necessarily know that I was doing this, but I was. Many times I felt His presence, as if He stood before me waiting. His presence terrified me. I didn't understand why I was being pursued.

God did give me what I wanted. I wanted skills to get a good job, and He guided and directed my path to a school in Newton, Massachusetts. After a year of training in secretarial skills, I applied for a job to be a secretary at Boston University. I was the assistant to the secretary of the President of the school.

Wayne was fully in the life of our child now. He cared for her on Tuesdays, and every other weekend. We were a good team, both madly in love with our daughter.

One of my teachers from the school in Newton called me one day. "How are doing in your job?" she asked.

"I really don't like it. It's boring," I said.

"I have a job for you that is anything but boring. Of course, you'll have to interview for it, but I have full confidence that it's yours, if you want it," she said. "It's a company that works with financing boats and airplanes," she said.

I did get that job, and it was a lot of fun. Yet it was extremely difficult working on Lewis Wharf and living in Brookline Village. At this time, Meg and I moved into our own little apartment. So, early we would rise. I would dress Meg and myself, put her in the stroller, and take off for a bus stop four city blocks away. Once we stepped off the bus on the other side of Brookline, I had only about three blocks to walk to my babysitter's house. She had a daycare in her home while her husband went to school. After Meg was settled, I walked several blocks down to catch the trolley I would take to Faneuil Hall and then on to Lewis Wharf. I was usually on time, but it was a long day.

I worked at the Wharf for a couple of years before I decided to return home. I was exhausted. I felt like I was robbing Meagan of myself. I dated in Boston one fellow I found to be dashing, handsome and exciting. But he had no room for my little girl. So that was that. Another unwanted heartbreak. The job was demanding and getting more and more complicated with boat shows and travel. So I moved home with my mother.

Moving from a big city of Boston to my mother's home in Red Lion, Pennsylvania was not a good idea. I went bar hopping way too much, while living at my mother's home. I was searching for something. What? I had no clue. I was a walking dead person.

The job in Boston on the Wharf called me and asked if I would be interested in moving to Olde Saybrook, Connecticut, where the vice president of the company had started his own business. I would be doing the same thing, but in Connecticut, which would be slower in pace.

I found a little place, clean and cute, a few streets away from the ocean. I enrolled Meg in kindergarten and went to work. I worked alongside of the boss' sister-in-law, who had a position of authority. I disdained her. I hated her way of training. I felt as if she had a demeaning attitude and had criticized everything I did. I kept making stupid errors, and in hindsight, she had every right to reprimand me.

One day I flipped out. "You're such a bitch. I cannot stand the way you manage. And I moved here to be pushed around by someone like you?" I said.

I was fired for speaking that way to the boss's sister-in-law. I was a woman filled with rage – empty - no peace, and now I had no confidence in my ability to work and properly take care of my child. No one wanted me. Not even a job.

I searched for another job and found none to be had. My boss refused to say to unemployment office he fired me; so I couldn't collect any funds. I applied for welfare in Connecticut, but time pressed and soon we were living on change. Wayne now was involved with a woman he recently met and announced their wedding plans. I was sick.

One weekend, Wayne had taken Meg, and I was alone in my rented house. Rent was coming up, and I had no way of paying it. I moved around robotically doing the household chores. I had just gone down to the basement where the washer and dryer were located. My thoughts were on Meg who was with Wayne and Maureen now. She's better off with them. Maybe I should give her to Wayne. At least she would be in a stable environment. She's young enough to forget me. I climbed the stairs, and about midway between the basement and first floor, I looked over to the ceiling beams. In my mind's eye I saw a hanging noose.

A voice said, "Do it! She's better off without you. You can't take care of her."

I paused, continuing to look at the noose, when another voice said, "Do you want to end your life and go to hell? Is that what you want?"

I ran up the stairs, flung my body down onto the bed and cried. I wept for hours. I cried out to God, "Help me. I'm sorry for what I have done, everything I have done. Please forgive me. Please help me."

I fell asleep, and the next morning I had a call from my sister Kelli. She was newly married and living in Harrisburg. "Nikki, will you and Meg come live with Don and me? Live with us until you get back up on your feet."

I cried. "Yes, Kelli, we will." Kelli reached me at my brink. How did she know? I will never really be sure, but I am thankful that she offered their help.

My two sisters were now married happily to men that they fell in love with and settled near Mom in PA. Jody was the first to marry and recently Kelli. Witnessing their happiness increased my loneliness. Jody's brother-in-law, Tom, was in town from Colorado visiting for the holidays, and offered to help me move by coming to Connecticut with his parents' station wagon.

I was packed and ready to go. I had written a sad, long note of explanation to my landlord asking him to please forgive me of my ineptness and my inability to maintain our lease agreement. I made sure that the house was sparkling clean and the heat turned to the lowest degree so the pipes would not freeze. And off we went.

Tom followed me as we drove through Connecticut, New York and then New Jersey. We were coming up to a bridge close to the Pennsylvania border. I was careful to go the speed limit for I feared being cited on my expired Pennsylvania inspection sticker. Meg slept peacefully in the back seat. My car was loaded with stuff, as well as the wagon behind me.

I saw a state policeman speed past me onto the bridge. He angled his car in front of a van ahead of me to stop traffic. Oh boy, is this guy in trouble, I thought. I, of course, was stopped and watched the police officer talk to the van's driver for a moment or two. It then drove away.

The policeman came up to my window and said, "Get out of the car, ma'am."

"What is it, Officer?"

"I said get out of the car right now."

Meg poked her head up and said, "Mommy, what's the matter?"

I grabbed her and pulled her up over the seat and said, "Come on, honey."

"Leave her in the car," the officer said.

I got out and saw Tom up against his wagon, spread eagle and being frisked. There were four other police cars parked around us now and policemen pointing rifles at us. "What's happening here?" I asked. It couldn't be for the expired inspection sticker.

"Tell me where you are going, who is the man you are traveling with, and what is he to you?" he asked. There was another policeman at the car window talking to Meagan. I told him everything. He then went over to Tom and asked him the same questions. We were then let go.

Apparently Tom looked exactly like a felon who had shot and killed a Boston policeman, and I looked like the girlfriend. The only thing that didn't fit was the child. The girlfriend had no children.

Could my life get any more bizarre? Of all things that I was experiencing, I now look, like a criminal.

CHAPTER 9
A PRINCE

Meg and I lived with Kelli and her new husband for a winter and worked for a temp agency until I found a 'real' job. Sadly it was that winter, while living with Kelli; I attended a friend's husband funeral. Denise and Scott were married for only a couple of years before he was diagnosed with cancer.

Denise had an infant son and invited us to live and share the expenses of her home. The little white house was located a mile or two from the hospital, where I was hired in the Public Relations department, and just two blocks from an elementary school. She offered to watch Meg after school each day until my day finished at 4:30 p.m.

I think she thought that the two of us would be of help to one another. She was one that brought stability, and I brought her comfort, in her dark days of grief.

As a natural blonde with high cheekbones, intelligent green eyes, a quiet manner with a sharp sense of humor, I found Denise to easy to live with. One night after the kids were in bed, she and I sat across from one another while drinking a beer.

"Denise, do you think you will ever re-marry?"

"I love being married. I can't imagine that I wouldn't," she said. "Once Justin is in school, I'll go back teaching. Of course, I'm not planning on it anytime soon."

"What about you, Nikki?"

"Yes. I'd like to be married but there just isn't anyone out there," I said.

"Let's make a list of the qualities in a man that you want to have for a life-long partner," Denise suggested.

"Well, ok. Let me think." I raised my beer to take a long sip. I picked up another Marlboro and lit it. "Do you want one?"

"No, thanks," she said. "But I do need another beer." As she walked over to the kitchen, I thought about the past, present, and future. I thought about my dad and some of his qualities that I knew I didn't want. I thought about my first husband and Wayne. I knew I needed clarity… maybe a list would help me.

"I want someone that is responsible and faithful. He's got to be trustworthy. He needs to be a hard worker, someone that I can respect. He needs to make a good wage. Or at least, have the potential to earn a good income. He's got to be smart."

"What else?" Denise asked.

"Ummmm, not a druggie or an alcoholic, and he can't be any kind of pervert. I can't have someone who would hit me either. He must like kids, of course. He has to have a sense of humor. I can't imagine living with a man for the rest of my life without laughter."

"And I'm not really a sports person, but it's wholesome. I wouldn't mind if he was somewhat of a jock," I added.

"What about his looks?" Denise asked.

"He should be handsome, yet not too pretty. I can't stand the kind of men that are always looking at themselves in the mirror. Yuck."

"How about religion?" she asked.

"Well... I don't know," I said.

"You don't care if he's a Christian or not?" she asked.

"Well, I guess. I never really thought about it."

"That will be priority number one on my list. Scott was everything I wanted in a man." Denise suddenly had a far-away look. "I can't imagine that there is anyone out there that will compare."

"Whoever it is, I think he will be special. No comparison to Scott. He will be his own person. Make sure he will be a good daddy to Justin," I said. "That's what I would worry about."

Denise and I were pretty good housemates. We were sensitive to one another's needs for privacy. If she wanted to go out or I had something to do, we were happy to stay with the kids. I don't remember doing it too often for her. She was healing and it took her a long time before she wanted to go anywhere solo.

My job at the hospital was boring. It was long hours of doing nothing. I would clean out drawers and shelves to occupy my time. Learn more about my word processor or work on the internal newsletter called *The Platter Chatter*. I would type the writer's articles for a monthly release or newspaper publications, but for the most part I was totally bored.

One afternoon, I sat with a cigarette in hand, thinking about my future. "When are you going to live for me?" a voice asked.

"When I'm married, God, I will live for you then," I said. Why I answered the question like that I do not know. Why I didn't freak out when I heard His question, I don't know.

It was just so natural. Nothing about His voice was spooky. And I didn't think about it again until a year or so later.

One day I got a call at work from Denise. "Hey, some guy dropped off a present for you. Do you know a Bill Arnold?"

"Yes. He's one of the guys I met a long time ago through my friend Roxanne. He asked me out to lunch the other day. He said he was in the area for business and he didn't want to eat alone. He's a nice guy. What did he drop off?" I asked.

"A watermelon," Denise giggled.

"A watermelon? That's weird. But who knows. We're just friends so he might have thought the melon was a nice treat for the four of us."

Bill Arnold seemed to have a lot of business in our town lately. He even had a relative in the hospital one week.

"I'm here to visit my ex-wife's grandmother. Can you break for lunch?" he asked.

At lunch I quizzed Bill on his two boys and his relationship with them. "I hate not being home to tuck them in at night or help them with their homework. It's really been hard these last couple of years."

"Oh? Are you still hoping to get back with your wife?" I asked.

"No. It's over. I mean, I tried for a long time to make it work, but she wasn't willing."

Once we got back to the hospital, Bill went to visit his grandmother. It was about an hour or so later that I walked out of my office to run an errand. There at the end of the hall was Bill. He was turning left, then right and then back again. He was obviously lost. I laughed out loud while I watched him circle. "You need to show him the way out," a voice said within my heart.

Bill Arnold was the man that fulfilled my list. And I didn't really even know it until Bill stopped coming around.

"Nikki, don't you think that Bill Arnold is the one you want?"

"He's just a friend, Denise."

"Think about the list you made with me a couple of months ago," she said.

I was stunned. My mind quickly went over the list. Yes, he was smart, handsome, funny, responsible, a good father, had a good job, wasn't an addict of any kind… and I let him go? I couldn't imagine he and I being an "us."

"I'm going to call my friend Rox," I said.

I asked her to have Bill call me and that was the beginning of our relationship. We moved in together within months, and then married within the year.

Bill and I loved our kids with all of our hearts. I loved Meg with all my heart and he loved his boys with all of his heart. Blending our family was hard and nearly impossible. But one day, before we were married, we discovered I was pregnant with the baby who would blend our two families into one. It was then we were married.

CHAPTER 10
MOTHER OF TWO

"We're in our eighteenth hour with contractions still coming every three to four minutes. Doc says he's going to hook her up to a bag of psilocin if it goes much longer," said Bill with his left ear planted to the phone as he watched me writhe from side to side. "I guess this is why they call this labor."

"Why don't you get off the phone? Stop announcing my labor like it's one of your basketball games." Bill's years of announcing sports on the local television channel and radio had invaded his everyday speech.

"Why don't you lie down on the couch for awhile? You must be exhausted," I said. I didn't want to be snappy with him but I needed a break.

"I'm more hungry than tired," he said.

"Hello, you two. How are we progressing, Nikki?" Dr. Jackson walked past me to the end of the bed. Before I could answer he stretched his latex glove onto his hand and used his fingers to check my cervix. "Ah, you haven't moved one centimeter... I think it's time for you and Bill to take a walk. Looks like you're here for the night," he said.

"Great! When can I have an epidural?" I asked.

"Not yet, it's too soon. I promise as soon as you reach six centimeters I'll get you one," Dr. Jackson said.

"Good. I don't like the sound of the woman in the next room."

Bill laughed, "Yeah, she's a screamer." The doctor laughed as he made his way out of the room.

"Are you ready? Help me up, will you?" I asked. Bill and I walked the halls of the maternity ward, hungry and tired. We passed a serving cart with a silver tray resting on its top.

"This must be dinner. I'm so hungry! Wonder what the hospital is serving tonight?" My husband made his way over to the cart and lifted the round silver cover, "UGH! Look at that meat – it's raw!"

Stitches of pain needled my sides, but at the same time I nearly fell down with laughter. "That's not meat; it's a woman's placenta!"

Back in the birthing room, hours trudged into the night while psilocin dripped ever so slowly into my arm. Punishing pain buffeted my abdomen every two minutes, yet my cervix had at last dilated to the desired six centimeters. "Oh help," I said. "Nurse, please, it's time for the epidural. The doctor promised."

"I'll go get the anesthesiologist," the nurse said.

The room was empty of any hospital staff. My groans grew louder and Bill rose up off the couch. His eyes were only slightly opened, his stand uneven. "The Lord is with you."

"What's going on with you, Bill?" I thought.

Unfortunately, the anesthesiologist did not arrive in time for me to receive an epidural. He was next door with another woman who had an emergency c-section. Twenty-six hours of labor and our baby girl was born at 5:10 p.m. on December 7, 1985.

"Look at her hair – she looks like Mr. T! Hey little girl, I'm your daddy," Bill cooed. "Stephanie Lee Arnold we are so happy you finally joined us."

Dr. Jackson asked for the anesthesiologist to give me something for the removal of my placenta. "She's been through enough. Let's put her under for the rest of it."

Bill left the hospital to be with Meg at my sister Jody's home. "Let me go see Meg, eat a bite and celebrate with a beer. I'll be back as soon as I can."

I faded off into a deep sleep. I woke with a start. I was in a different room with a nurse at my left side and her back to me. She was cleaning instruments.

I couldn't breathe. My throat was closed shut and I wasn't getting any air. I slapped my hand on the gurney for the nurse's attention. She swung around and asked, "What's the matter?"

I pointed at my throat with a face that had turned purple.

"Oh no," the nurse said. "Get a doctor in here!" She placed an oxygen mask over my nose and mouth.

I pushed it off for it was doing no good.

"Get a doctor in here, now," the nurse yelled.

Is this it? I'm going to die on this gurney. Where will I go? I will go to hell, I'm sure. I twisted this way and that trying to get a breath before I passed out.

I woke to a tube down my throat and the doctor asking, "Do you know your name?"

"Yes, it's Nikki," I said

"You scared the daylights out of us. Nikki, you must have had a reaction to the drug the anesthesiologist gave to you earlier."   Thank you God… I didn't die!

CHAPTER 11
CAUGHT

A frayed and faded yellow towel caught my attention in the wash basket at my side. "Another one bites the dust," I said aloud as I tossed it into the trash. "Why does his ex-wife demand so much from us and why does he never complain about it? His guilt strangles us financially."

Our newborn baby slept peacefully in her cradle nearby. A long sigh followed the realization that "even she couldn't fill the emptiness of my soul."

My eyes rested on the black face on our television screen across the room. Interest heightened as I looked at the man's face. What did he have that I didn't have? I turned up the volume to hear what he had to say, "He's not a God that sits way up high in the heavens with a long white beard like so many of us imagine. God is not a distant, disinterested being that hangs out in the cosmos somewhere and occasionally sees you. He's a God that loves you so much He sent His one and only Son into this world, not to condemn you but to save you."

My attention riveted.

"God's holiness demands payment for sin. We deserve hell…The Bible says that all have sinned and fall short of the glory of God. His standard is perfection. No one is perfect. Sin separates us from God. Therefore He sent His Son, God Himself, through the birth of a virgin. Jesus fulfilled the requirements of God's perfect law for us. He came for one reason to take your punishment and satisfy the debt you owe to a holy, just God. Now, He stands at the door of your heart to offer you eternal life. Jesus is a gentleman. He has given you a will and a mind to choose to receive this gift and will not come into your life unless invited."

I suddenly remembered the voice on the abortion table and the voice that called out my name in my bedroom, the voice that told me to run from danger, and the voice in my bathtub. With much trembling I asked, "Lord, if this is really true, please come into my heart. I believe. I want to believe. Forgive me, help me."

I reached for the huge coffee table King James Bible that my mother had gifted our family with at Christmas. "I am the way, the truth and the life. No one can come to the Father except through me."

For the next couple of weeks I asked over and over again for Jesus to come into my heart. I asked until I felt the Lord say, "Enough. I am with you."

Everyday I listened to the 700 Club and its testimonies. I listened to the teachings. I responded to their challenge of praying just fifteen minutes a day. I didn't feel different, just more aware.

During this time, I had been hired on a part-time basis to type manuscripts for a company in Lancaster, Pennsylvania. I picked up the manuscript to type while the baby slept when I had a quiet moment or two. The settings on for the computer were not right so it took time to get myself situated before I started typing.

I read the title page and set back in shock. "The Interpretations of the letters to Timothy and Titus."

"Bill, do you remember last week when we went to Reverend Shatto's church and we didn't understand it because the pastor was speaking about Timothy and Titus? Look at the manuscript I'm working on."

"Huh. What a coincidence!" Bill said.

I kept silent. I was beginning to see that God wasn't about coincidences.

After my manuscript was typed, I left Bill home with the kids to return it to the Lancaster office. I had the radio on and I was crossing the bridge over the Susquehanna River. I was about midway on the bridge when suddenly the car filled up with a powerful presence. His presence poured over me as rushing waters and He said, "I died for you. I DIED for you. I died for YOU." Tears rushed down my face. "I'm sorry, Lord. I'm so sorry Lord. What do you want me to do?"

On the radio a song by Joe Cocker came on and the one line that he sang was – *stand firm as a rock*. I changed the radio station and the same line of the same song was on. I for some reason changed the station one more time and again the same line of the same song – *stand firm as a rock*.

Peace showered over me in that car. It was as if a pair of huge hands steered the automobile so it wouldn't go off the bridge. Church steeples jumped to my attention as I left the bridge. Joy, joy, and more joy burst and bubbled up throughout my soul.

I delivered the manuscript to the office in Lancaster. Women, who were hard at work at their typewriters, stopped and stared. I wondered if they could see the cloud I walked on and His light in me. I knew I had stepped into another world.

CHAPTER 12
NEW LIFE

Now that I was a new citizen in this new world, I found that I no longer fit with my old habits. I didn't enjoy gossip, drinking or cigarettes as I once did. My mouth was no longer mine. In fact my entire personhood now belonged to someone else. Someone I wanted to know and please.

Even my relationship with my husband, children, mother, and father all had to be revised.

As I listened and repented of everything that God brought to attention, my friends and family took notice. I really didn't share too much in the beginning because I wasn't sure of my footing. But before the year was up, I had become a bold witness.

Bill could not figure out for the life of him what happened to the woman he married. I was unwilling to join him in our Friday night bottle of wine; I refused to watch offensive, violent movies, and of course I was uncomfortable with the normal parties with our old friends.

"I don't know where you are coming from," he would say. "I've been a Christian all my life. *I'm* the one who belonged to a Methodist Church growing up. For crying out loud, *I* was the president of my Sunday school class."

The more I tried to share with Bill, the more defiant he became. Our arguments were loud and crude. Everyday there was a stop for a drink after work, no matter how many times I demanded that he didn't. There was no conviction or thought about what he watched, said, or did. He lived his life for Bill Arnold and for sports.

Bill found me to be rigid and boring; and he was my prince who suddenly turned into a toad. I could see nothing good in him.

I had anger issues. I had a hard time resolving this escalating rage. I wrestled with guilt when I lost my temper with Bill.

Jesus lifted my nicotine habit. It wasn't easy but through dependence on Him I surrendered a two pack a day cigarette habit. Would God release me from this rage I had?

I learned how to fast and pray. I wasn't quite sure what the outcome would be. I knew I couldn't go on like this. "Lord, please. Help me. My anger is out of control. Something is wrong with me. Help me, please."

I was alone in my living room as Bill and the kids slept. "I love you, Lord. You are my God and I am your child. Thank you for rescuing me. Thank you for loving on me. Thank you for hearing my prayer. Thank you for your forgiveness."

My arms were raised in praise. I sought to bless my Father with all I could speak.

Suddenly there was a wind of warm breath upon my face. He had breathed upon me.

I wasn't scared, just curious. Later I read about the upper room experience in Acts and how the Lord breathed onto the disciples to receive the Holy Spirit. I really didn't understand it. I just knew I was pleasing Him with this act of worship.

The next afternoon during naptime, I knelt down to praise. I felt three strong forces being lifted off the back of my neck. "Thank you, Jesus. Thank you."

The Lord reminded me of a dream I had before I married, while I was living with Denise.

The Dream

I woke from a nap to three small human-looking things having a conversation between one another. The three were plotting my demise. The ringleader was a woman. Somehow

I knew that she was the most evil of the three. The other two demons were evil but more harmless. One looked to be a "dumb" spirit. He was so stupid I could barely stand it. The other was a manipulator. One who collaborated with the "female" to create the final destruction of my soul.

Now that the three forces were lifted off my neck, I had a calm demeanor. Not that I never lost my temper again, but I could see a major difference.

We had moved our family to Lancaster at this time and lived with Greenfield Estates, to be near Bill's job and boys. It was there that I befriended a neighbor named Wendy. She and I had children the same age and we walked together with babies in a stroller. I prayed for Wendy and her family and looked for an opportunity to share with her.

One day as we walked our babies, Wendy launched into a credulous story. "I have a friend I graduated from high school with and he's gone off the deep end. He says he has a personal relationship with Jesus Christ. Can you believe that? He told me that God even talked to him in an audible voice. What a nut!"

My heartbeat quickened and I knew a door of witness was being opened to me. "Wendy, I have to agree with your friend. I, too, have heard God speak. I, too, am a Christian."

I explained to her what happened to me on the bridge. Her eyes grew wide yet said nothing. That was the end of our walks.

It was on one afternoon, I went for a walk with my girls, mainly to get some quiet time away from my ever-distant husband. As I walked toward my house I saw Bill at our front door talking with Wendy. Wendy looked up and saw me. Her face cast downward as she scurried off to her own home.

"What did she want?" I asked Bill.

"Nothing. Nothing at all," he said.

I didn't have to wait too long before I knew what she said to Bill. In our next argument Bill said, "Let's move away from here. We need a fresh start. Even the neighbors are talking. I can't stand it anymore. Wendy said she's really concerned about you. She thinks you've lost it."

"I can't help what she thinks. What did you say to her in my defense? And what do you mean, move? Do you think I won't speak about Jesus if we move away?" I asked.

Rigidity attacked our marriage. He was unbending on his stand against change and I stood hard and fast in my new found principals. How was I ever going to relate to this man?

In prayer I begged for more opportunities to share the gospel while Satan used my husband, family, and neighbors to try and shut me up.

One morning I prayed, "Lord, how am I to go out into all the nations as you command? Will you show me how?" Within a matter of ten days, The 700 Club responded to a note I had written to Ben Kinchlow about how God used him in opening my ears to the gospel. They asked if I would be interested in sharing my testimony on tape.

I went directly to get council from a pastor's wife. "How much should I share?" Her large wise eyes watered as I spoke to her about my prayer request.

This woman's wisdom was renowned in our church. She had taught Bible studies, encouraging the body of believers to be salt and light wherever God planted us. "Bloom where you are planted," she would say.

"Nikki, what does Bill say about this?" she asked.

"He actually said it was ok with him, as long as he doesn't have to speak or anything."

"I would suggest you put it before your mother as a matter of honoring her feelings."

So that's what I did. "Mom, would you mind very much if I gave my story to The 700 Club? I won't speak about dad's crime or punishment. But if it's okay with you, I will tell about dad's alcoholism?"

"Well, half the world is an alcoholic, so it's okay with me," my mom said.

Once I had made the appointment for the camera crew to come to my house, I fretted about the whole thing. "Why did I agree to do this? I can't speak in front of two people, how am I going to speak on television?"

I was actually sick. I fussed over my home, my appearance, and my words. I shook when the interviewer asked me questions. His name was Nick, and I found him to be a bit dramatic. "Go ahead, let the tears flow," he'd say.

The heat of the camera was on my face and Nick would press me for more of my story. "I was ashamed of my dad's drinking and my parent's divorce."

I spoke of my emptiness, with the desire to end my life, and how hard my life was before Christ.

The interview went on for a couple of hours. The camera crew even took shots of my children and Bill playing a game at our kitchen table. I was surprised at Bill's cooperation and ease with the crew.

When my testimony actually aired there were many people who called my mother to say they didn't realize her ex-husband was such an alcoholic and how emotionally affected I was from the divorce.

Suddenly, I was the very, very black sheep in the family. My mother no longer remembered her permission she gave to me to air my testimony.

My family and I didn't speak to one another for three years. It was during this time that Bill left me for three months. He wanted to separate to see if we could work on our relationship while living apart.

I avoided my neighbor Wendy as much as any human could avoid another. I was hurt and angry with Bill that he allowed Wendy to say such things – his silence and desertion proved where his allegiance lay. And he didn't rescue or stand by me once my family heaped abuse upon me. Real hatred stirred in my heart for him and for my neighbor. He *left me* to live with his boss who is having an affair with his 19-year-old secretary. The dark cloud of divorce hovered over us.

One evening when Bill visited the girls, I went to a church service. I joined in worship and praise with a heavy heart. The pastor stood before the congregation ready to preach his sermon when he became silent. The young pastor stood at the podium weeping. He looked out into the fellowship of believers and said, "I had something entirely different I prepared to share with you but the Lord is speaking to me about the act of forgiveness. Please open your bibles to the book of Ephesians." I listened in awe about the importance of not giving the devil a foothold with bitterness. To forgive is freedom. He spoke about how God wanted no separation between us. When we withhold forgiveness there is division in your relationship with God.

The pastor said to call on those who have offended you and release them. Apologize for your actions and leave the rest to Him.

I went home and saw Bill. I spoke to him with sorrow about the things I have done and said that was uncalled for. I asked for forgiveness. Bill's whole demeanor was different. "Maybe we could go get counseling," he suggested.

"Yes, I would like that."

After Bill left me for the evening, I called Wendy.

"Wendy, I'm sorry for snubbing you in the parking lot. I Will you please forgive me?"

"Yes, I will. I couldn't figure out why you were treating me like that."

I refused to react to the indignation I felt and just agreed that I was the one in the wrong.

CHAPTER 13
A CHANGE OF THOUGHT

"The man is impossible to live with," I said to the counselor. "He doesn't like who I am in Christ. We don't have any common ground but our children and even then we are not on the same page in discipline."

"He says the same about you. Do you respect him?" Mr. Doder asked.

I looked at the heavyset man who sat across from me with raised eyebrows. "How? Just tell me how to do this? He leaves me to defend myself in every situation. Before Bill moved out, I felt we were the laughingstock of the neighborhood. Our arguments were so loud and out of control. He lies to me all the time. I keep telling him to be a man and tell me the truth. And, he moved out to live with his boss at work who left *his* wife and two boys for a 19-year-old girl. Bill and his sons ridicule me when I go to church at night or on Wednesdays. He hates the church I go to because the people give testimonies about God's work in their lives. He doesn't like to be around me, yet he doesn't want to live without me either.

"All I want to do is love the Lord with all my heart, soul, mind and strength and my neighbor as myself."

"That's impossible, don't you agree?" he asked. Mr. Doder swiveled his chair away from his desk and folded his arms onto his belly.

"Why would God tell us to do this if it's impossible? I mean we need His help with the Holy Spirit but it must be possible if He commands it?" I asked.

"I want you to read scriptures about what God thinks about divorce and marriage," he said while handing me a sheet of paper. "Please pray and may the Lord guide you."

"What about him?" I asked.

"He is instructed to read a book called, *Born Again* by Chuck Colson."

Okay, maybe God will work in Bill's heart through the book. In the meantime, I'll do my part by reading the scriptures.

Our separation was hard. I harbored resentful feelings toward Bill. "Who does he think he is, Lord? He's got a lot to learn about women and about you, Lord."

One night Bill came over to sit with Stephanie while I went to Meg's fifth grade concert where she played second chair as a violinist. I sat in the midst of couples, mothers, fathers, and grandparents, waiting for the curtain to rise. How I wished we had a family like these families around me. I looked longingly. "Why can't Bill see, Lord?"

The thick blue curtains rose slowly to the top of the ceiling. As it did, the Lord gave sight to my eyes. He showed me what He thought of me as Bill's wife. Suddenly, I saw a woman who sat way up high with a glance down onto my husband. I saw my critical, ugly attitude and heard my tongue slicing through any of my husband's attempts to find common ground. I saw my husband shrink back while I rode my high horse.

Sickened, I scurried home with Meg after the concert. I was so disturbed about who I was I could only nod to Bill as I made my way up to the bedroom. Bill for some reason followed. "What's wrong?" he asked.

I gulped back a flood of tears, "How can you stand me?" I asked.

Bill wrapped his arms around me and said, "Hey, we have our differences but we're still husband and wife. I still love you."

Our lives were on two different courses but I knew now what I must do. I must humble myself and elevate him. I must show respect and be sincere when I make compliments. "Oh Lord, please help me," I prayed.

CHAPTER 14
MY GOD, MY TEACHER

Unfortunately, I am a slow learner. My constant battle of living with an unsaved husband brought such deadness within our marriage. One night, when our clock chimed eleven times, I watched Bill maneuver to our bed and lift the comforter to snuggle close to me. I feigned sleep again, for another night.

I listened and waited for the familiar rhythmic breathing that accompanied his sound sleep. Finally, his soft snores became my signal to leave our bed. I walked onto the cushioned carpet through the hallway; groped through the darkened walls to find the banister that led me downstairs.

The nightly ritual of leaving Bill alone in our bed was what I would call "revenge." The argument three weeks ago was no longer valid but I stubbornly held my ground.

"Someday, it might dawn on him that I am a human being, not a doormat." I suspected I was treading on dangerous ground, but I no longer cared.

Tonight was particularly bad. Thoughts of leaving him swirled throughout my mind. A dark cloud settled over me as I thought about our kids. "How will they rebound if I leave him?"

Tired of thinking, I chose sleep as my favorite form of escape. I sank down into the crevice of the sofa and put my face toward its back. My sleep was fitful but I did sleep.

Sometime in the next hour, my eyes flew opened and my senses became electrified. Something or someone was in my space. I sought to fully wake up... I heard a laugh that raised the hair on my arms.

Hee hee hee hee

Ha ha ha ha

My heart pounded. Fear raced up and down my spine as I listened to the hideous laughter.

A deep voice resonated with evil while it boasted his victory over my marriage's destruction. Satan mocked me. I knew that I had played the fool. I had given Satan a foothold by going to bed with unresolved anger. Scripture flashed through my mind: "But if you do not do what is right, sin is crouching at your door; it desires to have you, but you must master it." (Genesis 4:7)

"Oh Lord, help me," I prayed.

Suddenly my body shook with a righteous anger. A flash of courage and strength carried my words into the darkness. "You shall not have my marriage; you shall not have your way here! For the Word of God says let nothing separate what God has joined together. You must leave Satan, in the name of Jesus Christ

The presence of evil vanished.

I raced upstairs and crawled next to Bill. I whispered, "Bill, I'm so sorry, please forgive me."

He grunted with acknowledgment that he had heard me. I pressed into his arm for him to wake.

"What's the matter?" he asked.

"I want you to know I am committed to you and our marriage," I whispered. "I'm sorry that I try to punish you for something you can't any remember you said or did. Please forgive me... I'm so sorry."

Bill did forgive me, again. And again we spent weeks of rebuilding what I had torn down and put our sights on purchasing our own home together.

Key West, Florida

Uncasville, Conn.

Kelli, Nikki and Jody

Our family in happier times...

An Easter Sunday when I was twelve years old.

CHAPTER 15
THAT ANCIENT SERPENT
CALLED THE DEVIL

"Lord, what am I going to do? I would like to be a part of the evangelism ministry at church, yet I'm battle weary thinking about it." I closed my Bible and set it on my nightstand.

Once I switched off the light, my knees rose to their familiar sleeping position, and I maneuvered a pillow to the most comfortable position beneath my head.

Unable to escape Dave Huber's voice earlier that day, I rolled his words over in my mind, "Come join us Nikki. Learn how to share the gospel through Dr. Kennedy's Evangelism Explosion class."

My life in Christ has not been easy. Family and friends thought I had gone mad. Open invitations to join their casual get-togethers were suddenly closed. Holiday gatherings were stiff mandates without joyous celebration.

My husband's rejection with a three-month separation, stung. Now that we have agreed to work it out and stay together, I frankly thought twice about going into battle again.

"Maybe, it isn't the right time to join the class, but whatever it is you want Lord, I'll do," I prayed and then fell into a deep sleep.

Sometime into the night, I woke with a start, aware of a presence in my room. Bill was away on business trip, or was he? Heightened senses caused the hair on my arms and head to stand at attention. Beads of sweat marched across my brow, while the heart muscle stretched in turmoil within my chest. My squinted eyes tried to adjust the room of darkness. And then I found it. A tall slender shape perched at the foot of my bed. Fear gushed out a loud scream as I watched his flared neck and forked tongue slither in and out of its angular mouth. Slit-shaped pupils widened with delight as its prey, me and only me, sat frozen, unable to move.

The serpent pushed off his tail with great force and caused him to fly across the length of our queen-sized bed. Before it reached my head, the snake slammed into what

I calculated to be an invisible shield. Vibrated echoes shot throughout the room when the snake dropped to the floor.

Shaken, I turned on the light and sat in breathless moments, trying to recover a sense of reality.

With the Bible in hand, I opened up its pages to Psalm 33; "But you are a shield around me, O Lord."

The next morning, I signed up for the evangelism class.

A DREAM

I soared high above the world and was filled with great joy in my view of rolling green hills and a blue sky. Suddenly I saw Him. He on a hillside and motioned me to come land. I stood before Jesus when He said to me, "It's about time you got here." His tone of voice seemed agitated. "Now go back and get some more."

"Oh Lord, yes, I'll go back and get a lot more people," I said.

He said, "No, you won't. You will get some but not a lot of people."

The next thing I knew I was in an airplane being instructed by the pilot in how to fly the plane.

I woke up with a start and wondered what the dream could mean.

On the first night of the evangelism class we were told to view a short clip of Dr. James Kennedy who was the creator of the Evangelism Explosion program that I was now taking. To my great surprise the first thing Dr. Kennedy said was, "Evangelism is like learning how to fly an airplane, once you know the mechanics of the plane or the gospel, you will know how to fly or present the gospel.

Of course Jesus was right. I did bring a few to the Lord through the EE program, but at least I learned the mechanics of the gospel and in turn built within me a lifelong confidence in sharing with others. The first person I had the privilege of leading to Christ was Greg. After Bill moved back home he kept in contact with Greg who by this time had also become my friend. One day I fussed at the Lord and said, "Lord, through this EE program I have witnessed to several people but haven't led one person to you by prayer." It was the same day that my phone rang and Greg said, "Okay, I give up. Tell me how to become a Christian." To this day I hardly remember how I led him in prayer but it has been years since. He repented and asked his wife for forgiveness and reconciliation. She refused to reconcile. Greg married the nineteen year old and she birthed him seven children. They have raised all the children in the church.

The more I learned about the gospel and how to share my faith, the more distant I felt from Bill. He stubbornly and persistently refused to look up or inward. So I kept quiet, hoping not to cause more of a division between us. Yet he had eyes to see and knew I was growing in leaps and bounds spiritually.

I tried to train up my children spiritually without him. I prayed with both girls, shared what I was learning and pointed out Christ to them in our daily walk. I didn't do this in front of Bill unless it was necessary. My youngest daughter Stephanie was now old enough to articulate faith. She would announce and proclaim loudly when she would see God's hand at work. Meg was a bit quieter but I knew too she had the seed of faith within her.

It was during this time when Meg was in the 8th grade when all that we knew to be true would be tested.

"What do you expect us to do about it?" Bill yelled across the dinner table. I cringed. I knew he wouldn't understand. Lord please, help me. I can't fight the school and Bill too.

"Don't you understand that the English teacher is not only reading questionable stories to Meg and her class, but he has invited the kids to come to his house at night. He says the ghosts speak to him there. Did you know that Mr. Sweat is a high priest at the Metro Church in Lancaster?"

"You're going to do what you want anyway – just keep me out of the middle of it," Bill sighed.

I looked over a Meg's face. Her long lashes were cast down.

"Meg, do you understand why we have to go to the school about this? I asked.

"Yes."

Meagan brought Mr. Sweat's weird stories and invitations to get in touch with the supernatural to my attention one afternoon when I questioned her on an unusual mediocre grade she received on her English exam.

"I want you to do me a favor; get written notes from the students from some of your classmates. I think it's important that I hear from them as well. For the time being, I'll get copies of the stories and read over them. I need to read these stories and see how bad they are before I go to the principal."

The next morning, I went to the Conestoga Valley Junior High to ask for the copies of the stories that Mr. Sweat had been teaching from. My new friend Lori Meredith is a teacher and encouraged me to do it this way. Lori was my first friend at the church we agreed to attend together as a family.

Standing before the secretaries and a math teacher's furrowed brows; I was given the copies of the stories without comment.

"Whew, Lord. I'm glad that's over with. Thank you for Lori's prayers and encouragement," I prayed.

I went home and spread the stories over my kitchen table. I read all of the stories and found three of them to be the opposite of anything I would ever teach my own children.

I pushed the story away in disbelief. Why would Mr. Sweat teach these stories?" One story was about a demon that demanded murder from the one he possessed. Human brains kept the demon named Enoch alive. The police authority or any who resisted him, he would kill. The story ends with the demon and the man he uses leaving the jail cell happily into the night.

I fell on my knees. "Jesus, I know that you brought this out into the light for a reason. Thank you for using Meg to share with me what's happening in school. Now tell me what you want me to do. I'm scared. Don't let me go into this without your help. Rise up your people to stand with me."

Bill agreed to go with our Youth Pastor Chris Labs and me to the principal's office at the Junior High School.

The young principal's eyes narrowed with suspicion. I voiced our concerns and objections to the stories. "These stories have no literary use, as far as we can see. The content is on murder without consequence. It's not just the Enoch story but also the other story telling of an accidental killing with no need to confess. What is this all about?"

"Mrs. Arnold, I'm surprised at your objections since we never experienced a problem with this curriculum in ten years. Oh, excuse me, there was one family - I believe they were Jehovah Witnesses."

"I wonder how many of the parents know about these stories since they are not given to the kids in a book to bring home," I said.

"We don't believe that our objections are so unusual," said Pastor Labs.

"So what are you going to do about this?" asked Bill.

"Listen; there isn't anything I can do. I suggest you take it to the school board."

"And how do we go about that?" Bill asked.

"You need to write a letter addressing the board stating your complaints and then you may approach the board at their next meeting."

We left his office perturbed but resolved to follow through with his instructions. I made copies of the stories and met with other women who had children near Meg's age. I asked them to pass on the stories to all of residents of the CV school district.

We had a petition signed by hundreds of people to protest the stories. Deb and Barb, concerned mothers in our school district, diligently sought signatures and made calls.

Four hundred and fifty people followed Bill and I to the next scheduled school board meeting. Bill jumped into the front lines. He was smooth as butter in his presentation to the board. I had written the required letter to the board, but Bill by far was the orator in the family.

The board members were taken aback with the huge attendance and decided to call a special meeting just for this hearing. Bill Arnold was scheduled to be at the auction's home office in Atlanta, GA for a manager's meeting on that very night.

"Bill you can't leave me. I can't speak before two or three people without freezing up. I stumble all over the place," I cried.

"I feel terrible but this meeting has been scheduled for weeks. I just got this position at the auction. I can't say no.

Besides the Pastors will be there and the other parents will stand behind you."

"Lord I am beyond scared, please help." I said.

The day Bill left for Atlanta, my phone rang incessantly. My friend Lori called and said, "Nikki, I am praying for you. How are you?"

Lori's children were my Steph's age. The kids got along and Lori was becoming someone I could trust more and more. "I'm okay. But this is going to sound weird to you. So forgive me but I need to tell you what happened. There was a truck in front of me carrying several large pipes. For some reason I felt that I needed to hang back from the truck's rear. Pipes shot right out of its back and barely missed my car. I feel like I'm in the middle of a war-zone. And it has nothing to do with flesh and blood."

Armed with Lori's prayers and the bodies of my brothers' in Christ, I walked through the auditorium doors of the high school. Two television cameras with their reporters were there getting comments from the board and some of the opponents.

"I will not talk to them. I can't. They are going to portray me as a fanatic," I said.

My friend and co-laborer Chuck leaned over and whispered into my ear. "No comment. Just say no comment."

The president of the board called the meeting into order. Mr. Silverman at the podium microphone proceeded to speak about the board's promise to answer our questions and concerns. I was the first one asked to speak.

"Chris," I whispered, "I can't. I cannot speak in front of all these people."

"Read your letter to them. Read," he said sternly.

I grabbed the letter I had written to the board and spoke into the microphone before me.

Our understanding of the meaning of education is to cultivate and discipline the minds of those that are placed under the school system's care. Cultivating these young minds requires the education's system to care, train, foster, build up and discipline. Discipline, as we understand it, is to improve the behavior of those that will enhance our nation's principles.

I felt the heat of the camera's lamp on my face along with the many pairs of eyes watching me. And I knew full well that there were many friends and just as many foes.

I drew in another breath, gaining more confidence even under the hate I saw from the president of the board himself.

We, as parents, take this job seriously and trust that our schools with its teachers to do the same.

The following stories do not promote this thinking and we find them most objectionable.

Enoch, written by Robert Bloch, copyright by Weird Tales 1946, reprinted by Scholastic Scope Magazine.

Enoch, a demon, living on top of a man named Seth's head. Seth explains the punishment and rewards of listening or not listening to the demon. Great rewards given to Seth when he would obey by killing human beings for Enoch – he receives an out of body experience and is promised to be a king in other lands. Seth explains that his mother, a witch, arranged Enoch's care over him after her intended death. Once Seth is arrested for nine murders, the District Attorney feigns sympathy for him for a full confession. Seth tells him everything. Seth fears Enoch if he does not kill for him, that he himself would be killed. The DA suggests that Seth give Enoch to him and he'll deal with him. Enoch eventually ends up eating the DA's brains since the attorney was unwilling to kill as Enoch demanded. He eats the brains of all those Seth kills for him. Seth and Enoch escape from the jail and they go out into the night – end of story. No repercussions for the murderous crimes committed.

Bloodstain, by Christopher W. Rowan, American Prefaces

This story is about a young man named Fred. Fred takes his father's gun without parental permission. Fred meets Mr. Haskell; whish is his best friend's father. Mr. Haskell warns and teases Fred about the gun...they part company. In a meadow, an hour later Fred accidentally shoots and kills Mr. Haskell. Fred agonizes over the death of Mr. Haskell throughout the rest of the story – until the end. Fred makes a final decision not to confess his guilt. Fred's mind was full of a strange and sorrowful peace and the assurance that he was safe...he resolved never to tell his secret. What is this story teaching our kids? Is it teaching our children that their minds can overcome guilt?

Examination Day, Henry Sleassar, HMH Publishing co., Inc. Playboy Magazine.

Dickie turns 12. The Jordon's inform their son there is nothing to worry about but must be tested by the government on this particular day. An examination is given and Dickie scores too high...he must be executed. Are we teaching our children that it is dangerous to excel in academics?

We believe that Conestoga Valley Schools has the power to shape and mold the minds of our young people. The children need to be built up, disciplined and trained to want to do what is right. To seek truth and abide in it. When we, the parents, schools, media, project violence, give out hopelessness and condone spiritual evil material – are we surprised that our children are not capable of any enhancement of the principles that this nation was founded on?

I looked to the center of the board's table where I met narrowed eyes and dark scowls across several of the faces.

We look to you the members of the Board of Conestoga Valley Schools, the caretakers of our children's minds, that you do what is right. We ask you to please remove these stories from the curriculum and replace them with literature that teaches the importance of truth and the maintenance of justice in regards to all moral offenses.

I sat down and the English teachers stood in defense of the right to teach what appeals to him or her within the guidelines given by the NEA.

One by one the audience stood up to voice their objections and questions about the material. One woman stood up and said, "What literary value are any of these stories? I have an uncle who is a Professor of English at UMass and he questions the teacher's intent."

Pastor Chris Labs stood up and came to the podium. His lanky body and pleasant smile turned toward the camera. "I am the Youth Pastor at Westminster Presbyterian Church and many of your kids are my kids. Kids, as you are well aware, are impressionable. They will try to get away with anything they can. That's the nature of our human heart. When you teach material about demons and their rewards for evil and no consequences from their wicked deeds, who knows what can spin out of all of that. Let's grant our kids good material to read with standards that their parents are in agreement with."

"Censors!" a male's voice screamed.

"Aren't we all censors? Do you encourage your children to read pornography so that will be enlightened?" asked Chris.

"That's ridiculous," one female board member said.

On and on it went. The final decision came days later. The board decided to take the story of Enoch out of the curriculum, yet allow it to remain in the library. The other stories will remain, but the school would grant students the freedom not to read them.

The teacher was promoted to the administrative office of the school. And the parents of Conestoga Valley School District had a renewed commitment to their children's education.

Satan had his day with the bombardment of fear, accusations, interruption and unwanted publicity. My family, meaning sisters and mother, must have seen the news and I was certain that they were shaking their heads about my fanaticism.

Bill never wanted to tell his sons about our contending with the school board. I guess he originally thought it would not get back to them. Billy and Chris personally visited or stood up in college class to denounce this fanaticism of their parents. They were ashamed of our involvement. And I was ashamed of their standing against their own family for the ungodly principles of those in the school system.

Resentment and deadness cloaked over my heart against my husband. I began to question his 'meeting' in Atlanta, his decision not to tell the boys, and his initial reluctance to 'get involved.'

With this entire trial, I learned I have a choice. I can do what is right or open the door to the crouching sin that desires to have me. I am still learning how to master it.

CHAPTER 16
MANNA FROM HEAVEN

"Lori, I can't ask Bill to pay a hundred and eighty dollars for a pool pass. You know how we are trying to save for a down payment for a house. We keep wasting money on this townhouse, we'll never get out of here," I said.

A few moments of silence passed between us as Lori and I were on the phone. "It's going to the hottest summer in decades. Why don't we ask the Lord if He will provide the money for a pool pass? I know He will answer," said Lori.

"Lord, I ask you if you are willing, please allow us to belong to the same pool that Lori and her kids go to. I know it would be great fun for our kids but it is up to you."

The doorbell rang. "Hey Lori, I'll call you back. Someone's at my door."

Before I could get out of the kitchen, Stephanie's five-year-old spindly legs ran and flung open our front door. "Mommy, look at this!"

In her arms she carried a huge box. I saw the back of the UPS leave our parking lot.

"What is this I wonder?" I asked. I picked up the package and looked for a return address but there was none. I even had to search for our name and there was a small nametag, in the tiniest letters addressed to Mrs. Nikki Arnold.

"Hmmm," I said.

"Open it up Mom," Meg said.

I ripped open the package and found a large boom box radio. There was a note that said I have won a radio shack drawing. "I don't remember giving my name to any drawing," I said.

"It's ours now," said Meg.

"Yippee," said Stephanie as she jumped and down.

There was a still small voice that spoke to my heart. Use this for the pool pass.

I called Bill at work and told him about the prize and the request for a pool pass. He took the model number and called the Radio Shack to see how much it was worth. The auction bought it for a dealer's prize in the summer sale. Radio

Shack said the boom box radio was worth $185.00. And the Arnold's enjoyed a family pool pass with good friends that summer.

Ask and it will be given to you:
Seek and you will find

I slammed my pocketbook down, looked into my husband's eyes and said, "Why is it so hard for you to get me another car? Don't you understand how embarrassing it is that I'm married to an auto auction manager, and drive around in this piece of junk?"

Pain flashed across my husband's face.

"It not only looks bad, but smells of rotten egg," I said. "And please, please get that headliner fixed. The tacks keep falling out, and it's a lot of fun driving around with material on top of my head!"

Clenched hands, Bill stood up, paced our living room floor and with a raised voice said, "Do you think for one moment that I like this? Don't you think that I want to do better for you and the kids?"

"I think it isn't a priority. In fact, your company car is real nice, so you don't think about it much," I said. "I think that you need not worry about the noises, the stalls, the smell and everything else because you're not driving around in it. And on the rare occasion you are, for some reason it runs perfectly fine for you. So again, it's pushed back into the low priority file."

"And the car doesn't act up for the mechanic. Remember, it was serviced just three weeks ago?" Bill asked.

"Let's watch our tone of voice," I said. "No need for the smug attitude."

"All right. You quit your bitching, and I'll quit with the attitude."

I cringed and walked away. This conversation was going nowhere.

Bill followed me into our bedroom and said, "Look, it isn't the prettiest car, but can't you hold on a while longer until we get a little bit ahead?" His dark eyes pleaded. "Let's compromise. I'll get the headliner fixed, if you drive the car for another winter."

I suddenly felt bad. Swallowing hard, I said, "All right, I don't like it but agree to wait until spring."

Later that day, God spoke to me through His Word. "Do not be anxious about anything, but in everything, by prayer and petition, with thanksgiving, present your requests to God, and the peace of God, which transcends all understanding, will guard your hearts and minds in Christ Jesus. (Philippians 4:6 NIV)

At once I knew I was guilty. Guilty of anxiety, prayerlessness, grumbling, and shame crept over my bones. "Lord, forgive me of incessant complaints and the unreasonable anger I feel towards Bill. I'm sorry. Please help me to do things Your way."

One afternoon while driving on the traffic laden Route 30, thick smoke seeped through the hood of my brown bomb. I inched to the side of the road, aware of blaring horns of so many impatient people.

"Great," I muttered. "Now what am I going to do?"

A still small voice spoke, "You have a choice; you can fret and spew, or you can give me your anxiety and present your request with thanksgiving."

"Okay, Lord. Have it Your way. I cast my anxiety over to You, for I know that's what I should do. I ask you to help us to sell this old clunker. And let the next car be dependable, reasonably quiet, odorless, and any other color than this ugly brown."

Now to the business of applying His word further, I praised Him for all the blessings He has already sent my way. "Thank you for a clear day. Thank you for the nearby gas station, just a mile away. I praise you that my children are safe at home. Thank You for my husband who does care, is responsible, and manages our finances so well."

At home, I reported all that happened to Bill. I told him of the help I received from the mechanic at the station, and the minor problem of a fan belt that needed to be replaced. No complaints. No nagging, just a report.

To my astonishment, the sale of my car became Bill's number one priority, for the next several weeks.

"Nikki, I don't know what else to do. I've advertised it in the newspaper, posted a For Sale on the rear window of the car, and even sat it on the car lot a few times. I haven't anyone show one bit of interest in the car. I guess it's the market at this time of the year. Let's let it rest for awhile, take it out of the paper, and try again in the spring."

I agreed, but prayed, "It's your timing Lord. I know you can do anything."

On February 14, while ironing I prayed, "Lord, it is Valentine's Day. I have nothing for my husband. Please help me to come up with a creative gift that will be of no cost to our pocketbook. Forgive me Jesus of being so thoughtless..."

The telephone rang. "Hello, this is the Arnold's" I said.

"Er, am I speaking to the household that has a brown station-wagon for sale?" a male voice asked.

"Yes you are."

"Ma'am, my name is John Martin, and I'm interested in taking a look at your car. Can I see it today?"

"May I ask who gave you our phone number?"

"I drove by a car lot a few days ago and saw a brown station-wagon. It thought it might be what I'm looking for, but by the time I turned around, your car was off the lot. So I asked the fellow who works the lot if he knew the owner of the vehicle," he said in his Pennsylvania Dutch accent. "It is for sale isn't it?"

"Oh, yes," I said.

"Again, I would like to see the car today if it's okay with you."

Within thirty minutes I was on my way to the Lancaster Shopping Center where we agreed to meet. "What am I doing? Why didn't I call Bill to tell him about the phone call? Lord, please let this guy legit."

Once I reached the parking lot, I saw a middle-aged man who wore a warm smile and a gray derby hat.

I parked the car and got out. "Hi. I'm Mrs. Arnold."

He nodded at me as he looked over the car. "There here tires look to be in good shape." He opened the hood to study the motor. "It looks like the oil is pretty clean. Might I take it for a drive?"

Lines of uneasiness scampered across my forehead.

"You can come along," he said.

I nodded with a knot that settled in the pit of my belly.

We climbed into the brown bomb and he turned the key.

The putrid smell seeped through the heater vents, the car wheezed and groaned as Mr. Martin pressed the gas pedal.

A blush crawled across my face.

"How much are you asking?" he asked.

"Well, ah, my husband wants $1,550 for it," I said.

"Why do you say it like that?"

"Because of the smell, and all the noises within this car," I said. "But if you want to barter, you need to talk to my husband."

Mr. Martin stared at me for a few moments before he said, "Listen, I buy what the Lord directs me to buy, and he told me to buy this car. Don't you concern yourself about the noises for you see, I'm a mechanic, and there isn't really anything I can't fix. I'm buying the car for my son who is a youth pastor at an evangelical church in Myerstown.

That night John Martin called Bill, and the car was sold for $1,500. A few days later, I was the owner of a newer black car that proved to be dependable, quiet and odorless.

Now, could I trust Him for the purchase of a house without a down payment?

It was early in the fall season when we were shown a house by a friend of Bill's who was a realtor. It was an adorable Victorian style home, fairly new, in a development that would be perfect for raising our family.

"We can't afford this house," Bill said. "What I mean is, we could afford the monthly mortgage payments but we don't have the $7,000 needed for closing."

"Then why did Liz even show us this place?" I said in frustration.

Meg had a friend from school that lived only two blocks away from this house. "Maybe we shouldn't have enrolled Stephanie in Lancaster Christian School," I said.

"Nikki, I said we are able to make the monthly payments. That means we are able to keep Steph in private school," Bill said.

Bill and I worried about our youngest because of all the mess the year before with the stories that were being taught. Meg opted to stay within the public school system since she was an honor student and named captain of the school's tennis team. It made house hunting a little more difficult being that we needed to stay within the school district.

I went to prayer, as did the whole family, about the will of God. "If it is your will for the purchase of this home, please help us."

Bill got a phone call and it was his friend, Liz the realtor. "I decided, if you want this house, I will front you the $7,000 with a written agreement that you will pay me back when your bonus is given in the beginning of next year. Within five months we received a bonus from Bill's work and we were able to pay her back immediately.

We were amazed at God's generous Hand of provision. And our blessing gave us a short reprieve from marital problems. The excitement of decorating our new home, our new neighborhood, and a new puppy was fun but temporary. I was about to receive another painful lesson on 'Loving Your Neighbor'.

CHAPTER 17
STIFF-NECKED WITH STIFF CONSECQUENCES

My daughter held hands with her little friend Jennifer. "We're best friends forever," she said.

"That's nice Steph. I'm glad you two are buddies. It's good to have Christian friends. Everyone needs a best friend."

I loved my daughter's heart for those who needed friendship. Jennifer had needed a friend and Stephanie was more than willing to meet that need.

I thought of my friend Lori, and how she had accepted and loved me with all my warts and bruises. Lori came from a wholesome Christian family and loved me even though I did not. Lori committed herself with a vow as Jonathon and David has committed themselves to one another. I was happy that my children had good Christian friends as well.

Jennifer's parents drove her forty miles each day, twice a day to attend the Christian school of their choice. Jennifer's eight-year-old frame with curly brown hair and a weak chin didn't compare to my daughter's muscular athlete body. Yet, Steph enjoyed the role of protector against anything that might threaten Jen's equally sensitive personality.

On special occasions we would invite Jennifer to our home for a Friday night sleep over and drive to meet with her parents at the designated halfway point. One particular Saturday we decided to drive Jennifer the whole way home with an invitation from her parents to visit.

We didn't stay long. Blank white walls and awkwardly placed furniture within their townhouse made me even more uncomfortable with our already stiff conversation.

"Do you think they are in trouble financially?" I asked Bill after we got back into the car for our ride home.

"I can't judge a thing like that. Why do you ask?" he said in his voice of exasperation. "They send their daughter to a private school. They can't be hurting that bad."

"It's just that they offered us an iceless glass of warm water as something to drink," I said.

"If you wanted some other drink, you should have asked for it," Bill suggested. He was right. He had a knack of accepting and thinking the best of all that he met until proven otherwise. Why was I so judgmental?

One September I was asked to go along on a business trip to California with Bill. So naturally I thought of Jen's parents as the children would have a great time together and any homework or activities that needed to be done I knew Jen's parents would be able to see it through.

"Marilyn, if you could watch Steph for just three days, we will certainly return the favor one day when you and your husband want to get away," I said.

Marilyn hesitated. "Sure. We'll do that. Is there anything that I need to know about Steph?"

"No. She'll eat whatever you have for dinner. She's not allergic to anything but penicillin. I'll send some food along for her packed lunches. Bill and I really appreciate your help," I said.

The San Diego business trip was short and sweet. Bill had business and I enjoyed the sights of California for three days. Once we returned I sent flowers as a thank you to Marilyn and picked Steph up at school.

"How was your time?" I asked Steph.

"Good mom. Really fun," Steph said.

A couple of days after our return home, I felt the Spirit's urging to call Marilyn. The Spirit brought this woman to mind for a full two days. I knew He wanted me to befriend her. "No Lord. She may be Steph's best friend's mom, but I can't see me being friends with her. We have nothing in common other than our daughters. Besides, Marilyn and her family live too far away for any kind of friendship," I said with justification.

The next morning I went into Stephanie's school and sensed a cloud of despair in the hall between the parents. "Did you hear the news?" one mother asked me. "Marilyn, Jen's mother committed suicide in her garage yesterday. Apparently she suffered from depression for a long time."

Stunned in unbelief, I hurried to Stephanie's class and found her in tears. "Mom did you hear? Poor little Jennifer, what's going to happen to her now?"

After the funeral Jen's dad asked if she could spend a couple of days with our family. I witnessed sadness draped over Jen with sobs that broke our hearts. Stephanie immediately went into action by taking her under her wing and carried her burdens on her young shoulders. Jen and her father moved shortly after Marilyn's death to Florida.

I can only wonder if I would have obeyed the Spirit's voice and thought less of myself what might have happened and how much pain could have been avoided. If I could only been like Jesus, or Lori, or Stephanie.

CHAPTER 18
LOVE THY NEIGHBOR

Our new home sat in a development of manicured lawns and neighbors who seemed friendly enough, conscientious and for the most part, people who minded their own business.

Except for a little girl named Kelly.

Kelly was a pixie face nine-year-old who immediately made her way over to our home to check out the 'new kids on the block'.

"What is that?" asked Kelly.

"What does it look like?" I was a little miffed already. This kid had opinion about everything, even my furniture.

"Well whatever it is, you should throw it away." Kelly turned her attention to Stephanie. "Hey, do you want to spend the night?"

"Thank you Kelly, but she's a bit too young yet to spend the night at a friend's house."

"Mom, please," Stephanie begged.

"No, if Kelly wants to stay here, she can, but you are not spending the night at her house," I said.

With a wrinkled turned up nose, Kelly walked to our door. "You treat her like a baby."

"Listen girlie, for your information, Stephanie is three years younger than you are. Besides, as far as I can tell we will be neighbors for quite some time." I said with indignation.

"Boy, your mom's strict." With that final remark Kelly walked out our front door.

Later that night I said to Bill, "I don't know about that kid. Chuck and Cathy moved their family out of their neighborhood because of the bad influences with their kids' friends. Maybe we should have considered this predicament before we moved here."

"Aw give her a break, she's just a little kid. Anyway, how can you know anything more than what's on paper when moving into a new area," he said.

Meagan quickly adjusted into our new house and neighborhood. A friend from school lived around the corner, who happened to be a concert pianist, and an honor roll student.

Her parents had our values and though I did not know them personally, I knew the family had a fine reputation. I encouraged this friendship and watched Meg begin to challenge herself academically with a competitive nature.

But, my heart ached for Stephanie. The Christian children around the corner snubbed her friendship. They had enough playmates, as far as they were concerned. No matter how often the parents tried to ignite this friendship, our kids never clicked.

There was only one that pursued Steph's friendship – Kelly next door. Every day of the week, she appeared in our home at one time or another. I didn't mind her presence in our home as much as I minded her constant challenges of Christian values. "Why must you pray over every meal? Or "Why do you do devotions with Stephanie every day? Or "Why can't Steph watch this television show or that?"

It was through these questions that I learned that Kelly lived differently than we did. I learned that her mom, Kris, was a devout Christian but her dad was not. I saw the spiritual struggle within the home. Kris did not nag or try to arm wrestle with her husband about his lack of faith, but had waited patiently for the Lord to work. I can say I worked quite the opposite on Bill, and what a sorry mess I made out of things.

One October day, I overheard Kelly and Stephanie playing on our long front brick porch. "What are you going to be for Halloween?" Kelly asked.

"I'm not allowed to go trick or treating. I go to an All Saints Day Parade at my church instead. It's really fun. You should try it," Stephanie suggested.

"I'm a witch," Kelly declared. "I'm going to cast a spell on you."

"Hey, missy. We don't talk about such things around here." Here I was again, the party pooper, the mean old mom who wagged her finger at all the dos and don'ts of our Christianity. Why did this child always make me feel so small?

Over the years Kelly challenged me in all areas of my witness. It happened to be that Kris, her mom, asked me to open my home to her youngest daughter, Kelly, for an hour after school until she would get home from work.

"Ok, Lord. Help me to love her," I prayed.

Cookies and milk and times of play helped me to get to know Kelly better. She was a strong-willed child to say the least. Yet, there was a loneliness about her that tugged at my heart. Kelly was always at our door.

Summer mornings, I would get out my Bible to do devotions with Stephanie.

"Mom, can I invite Kelly to do this with us. She needs to know who Jesus is," she asked.

That was a beginning of spiritual stirrings and questions with the inquisitive child's mind that would not just accept everything on the surface. She needed to find out the truth. "How can anyone walk on water?"

"You're right. Only God can do that," I said.

"Is there really a heaven? And hell?"

"That's what it says in the Bible," Steph replied.

"So? What if the Bible is wrong?" Kelly would push.

"There are over 2,000 predictions of the future that have come true. No one can predict the future like that so accurately. But it is your choice to believe or not. We choose to trust what the Bible has to say. I believe it is God's love letter to each one of us."

At this point, I knew that the Holy Spirit was truly dealing with Kelly. I shared this with Kelly's mom.

"Kris, God is drawing Kelly to Himself."

Kris's eyes lit up. "Yes, I can see that. The new Youth Pastor is doing a great job. My prayer for so many years is that God would do whatever it takes to bring Kevin to

Himself. Maybe, our girls' faith will show Kevin, who knows. All I know is that God will answer my prayers when its time." Kris's beautiful face and calm demeanor reflected deep trust in His promises. "At least Kevin goes to church with us, even if he doesn't believe."

"That's good. Bill's taking baby steps. He's become a member, but too often I think he's caught between two worlds. You know what I mean?" I asked.

She smiled and nodded, "In His time."

Kris was someone I admired, and liked. Kelly, her daughter, was another matter.

The next few years were at times a challenge, until one night about 8:30 p.m. on a Tuesday evening, Kelly knocked on our door.

"Kelly? What are you doing here? Steph's in bed already."

"Can I talk to you Mrs. Arnold?"

"Of course, come in."

Fear and sadness crossed over Kelly's face. "Do you think I'm going to go to hell when I die?"

I leaned forward with my chin in my hands and raised an eyebrow. "What's going on in your life Kel?"

Tears slid down Kelly's cheeks as she struggled to get her thoughts in order and with a cough she cleared her throat before she said, "I fainted in school today, in the middle of algebra class. I fell off my chair, onto the floor, and right in front of Tommy Watson's desk. Wouldn't ya know that Tommy is the coolest kid in the whole school? UGH, talk about embarrassing. Anyway, Mom took me to the doctor's, and guess what? The doc said I have a bad heart."

"What? What does your doctor mean by 'a bad heart'?" I asked.

"He said I was born with it. I'm scared I'm going to die."

Once again, tears welled up in those beautiful green eyes.

"Oh Kel, if it's a heart murmur, it rarely causes anyone to die. Don't worry about that. But you're right, we all are going to die, sooner or later."

"I do bad things. It's not that I want to do bad things, but everyone in junior high does bad things."

I couldn't help but grin at Kelly's struggle. "Honey, don't you know everybody has that struggle. There's only one thing in life that makes anybody go to hell. That's not accepting what Jesus Christ did for you over 2,000 years ago on the cross. Jesus, who is God, the Son, came to earth for the purpose of taking our punishment for us... to satisfy God the Father's wrath. You see, after Adam and Eve disobeyed God, they brought sin into the world and passed it down to us. Everyone is born into sin and then we make our own choices to sin. No one is perfect. Only One is perfect and that is Jesus and He offers His sacrifice to the Father to take care of our punishment – all we must do is believe in Jesus and ask Him to come into your heart. He'll help you to do what is right. Can you trust Jesus with all you have?"

Kelly slid down onto our carpet and looked up at me. "I'm ready. What do I have to do?"

That evening, Kelly prayed and asked Jesus into her heart. It was a simple prayer of faith and trust.

I reported all of this to Kris the next day and encouraged them both to do devotions together.

Over the next couple of years Kelly's visits became sparse. The age difference between Stephanie and Kelly became more intolerable as Kelly grew and became more involved in school.

There was one summer day that clinched our frail contact forever. While I weeded my front garden, I looked up to see a teenage boy at Kelly's front door. I watched Kelly look to the left and then to the right, not at all noticing me on my knees in our garden. She opened her door and the boy scooted in.

Uneasiness crept up my spine, for I knew Kris and Kevin were at work and Kim, Kelly's older sister, too, was not at home. I quickly got up and went into my kitchen. I picked up my phone and called over at Kelly's.

"Kelly?"

"Yep, this is she," she said.

"This is Mrs. Arnold. Are you allowed to have boys into your house – when no one is at home?"

"Yes, I am," she said.

"Good, I plan on talking with your mom once she's off work."

Moments later, the boy shot out of the house.

Over the next couple of years, Kelly avoided me at all costs. If I happened to see her, she turned her nose upward and looked the other way. On an occasion I would see Kelly walk home from the bus stop or in the neighborhood with her friends. She had become a beautiful young woman with long curly brown hair, and quite a shapely figure. I noticed the boys and kids that came over quite a bit. The Bouman's house looked like a focal point for all teenage kids.

On September 16, 1999, at 4:30 p.m., the whole world stopped in our neighborhood in Brownstown, Pa., when a State Trooper with pad and pen in hand stood at my door.

"Hello. Can I help you?" I asked.

"I'm looking for a Mr. Kevin or Mrs. Kris Bouman," he said. "They're not at home and we're trying to locate them."

"Kris should be home soon. She works in Leola at a doctor's office, but I really don't know the name of the practice. Kevin works in Harrisburg and I have no idea when he's coming home. Why? Where are the girls? This doesn't have anything to do with their girls?" I asked nervously.

The trooper shifted his weight from one side to another. I thought I saw a tear in his eye. "We are not at liberty to speak to anyone before we speak to the parents."

I started to shake. I turned around and looked at Stephanie who was standing behind me. "It's Kelly, mom, I know it."

I knew it too. Was she hurt? Was she in the hospital? Arrested for some offense? I reasoned that Kim was older, but I never could see her in any kind of trouble. She was quiet, and unassuming; never pressed the limits. Kelly was a different kind of girl. She pressed every limit that was in existence.

Prayer chains started for the family, Kris' pastor was notified, and neighboring friends were weighed down with the worst anxiety.

Once Kris and Kevin were at home, the State Troopers were there for only a few minutes. "That's not a good sign," Bill commented.

Before long, two neighborhood teenage boys stood at my door. "We don't know if you heard or not but Kelly Bouman died today. She hitched a ride home with a friend after school. He was driving too fast and hit a telephone pole. She didn't have her seatbelt on and flew out the window. They say she died instantly." The tallest boy stared down at his sneakers. He swallowed back tears and said, "She was one of my best friends."

Our whole family was in shock and in tears. We hugged one another, and prayed for Kevin, Kris & Kim. We made our way next door to give our condolences to our neighbors. How I dreaded to look into their eyes and feel their pain. "Help us Lord."

We made our way through a maze of grieving relatives, friends, and teens. Some faces wore devastation, others were in shock, and still others had a strange peace.

Kris looked and saw me. She stood up and came over to embrace me. "Thanks for coming; I'm sorry you had to have the police at your house this afternoon."

"Oh my Kris, don't be sorry for us. God obviously wanted you and your family to be covered in prayer – immediately," I said.

"Kelly's with Jesus now. Nikki, a month ago Kelly re-dedicated her life to Christ in church – even stood up and gave testimony in loving Christ." Kris said with her eyes bright. "No doubt in my mind where Kelly is now." Kris then pulled me aside to a corner of her house to privately speak to me. "Remember my prayer to Jesus about Kevin. I asked Him to do whatever it takes to bring Kevin into the family of Christ. Maybe this is it," she said. "Pray for Kevin. How can you get through this without God?"

"I will… we will," I said.

Kris's face paled. She suddenly looked exhausted. I wrapped my arms around her and said, "Listen we're going to go, but if you should need anything, please let us know."

That night I wearily climbed our steps to the silence of my darkened bedroom. I sighed while undressing, grateful for time alone.

My silence was interrupted with moans outside. Wails of cries cracked through my coveted shelter. I carefully went to my window and lifted the edge of a curtain and saw young people standing in the middle of the road with arms wrapped around one another.

"Oh Lord Jesus, please comfort them," I prayed. A weary cloud of oppression hung over me, I sought Jesus after my family went on to their beds. I made my way to my knees; I had to climb into His peace.

"Lord, I praise you for Kelly and the knowledge that she is with You. I thank you for that assurance, yet we are so sad for her friends and family. Please comfort them. Please bring Kevin into your arms of peace – grant him salvation through his daughter's death."

Three days later, our car purred into the parking lot of Kelly's church. Rain with dreary dark clouds descended upon Lancaster County that day. I thought it might be the reflection of God's own heart. We passed through a tunnel of sadness; grief-stricken and stone-faced people waiting to get into the church. The long line of people clothed in black – the color of death and the color of night. Those who were not in black were her teammates in soccer, and her co-cheer-leaders for football.

Each person made a way slowly to Kelly's family hugging, holding, crying and cajoling. Kris and Kim comforted each person with a word or hug. Kevin extended a warm handshake to each mourner – his face pale and strained.

Pictures were strewn throughout the sanctuary on poster board in commemoration of her short life. I was most taken with her pictures of when I first met her impish nine-year-old face. "Why did I feel such aversion to this sweet little face?"

All pews were filled. Other chairs were brought out for more to be seated. A hush settled over the crowd, as Pastor Wert made his way to the podium, where he monitored over the whole service. He introduced friends, teachers, cheerleaders, coaches, her youth pastor all gave a vibrant testimony of a girl who desired to live life to its fullest. 'A candle in the wind' by Elton John, was played on the piano by a friend – the boy's voice cracked on and off key, once he finished he said, "She would always bug me to play and sing that song."

Friends spoke of faithfulness, her kindness to each one. Cheerleaders testified to Kelly's trustworthiness. They could count on Kelly to catch them when they did their routine jumps. They vowed to cheer for Kelly at all future games.

Others got up and shared poems written for Kelly and another friend read an essay Kelly had written in English the previous year. The essay spoke of wanting to use all her talents and gifts to the utmost. She wrote that she wanted to live life to its fullest.

A blond young man with wire rim glasses made his way up to the podium and spoke confidently into the mike. "Hi, I met Kelly a couple of years ago. I was an atheist and Kelly told me about God. I'm no longer an atheist. And, if you're listening Kelly – thank you – I'm going to miss you."

Stephanie suddenly bent her head down into her lap and wailed. I put my arm around her and watched my husband's eyes swell with tears.

The Youth Pastor rose up and spoke. "Kelly was a good tease and always a lot of fun. I remember one night when we were having a sword fight with paper towel rolls and I accidentally swatted her in the face. I didn't mean to hit her in the face and she played on my sorrow by saying, 'it's ok, I'm going to tell the school that an old man at church beat me.'" Chuckles rippled throughout the crowd.

"On a more serious note, Kelly hurt her back on a recent youth retreat. I rode with her in the ambulance and stayed with her until all the tests showed she was all right. She told me, "I need to get right with God," said the Youth Pastor. He cleared his voice before swallowing hard, "Kelly was full of life and wanted all she could get. She may have tested the limits but she loved God."

Pastor Wert now was at the microphone with a raised hand holding Kelly's bible. As you can see, this is not an unused Bible. It is marked up and worn thin. She may have tested the waters, and may not have done everything right, but neither does anyone here – including myself. The Bible says, "All have sinned and fall short of the glory of God. And it also says because God so loved us – He sent His one and only Son – for Kelly, for you and for me – not to condemn us but to save us. Kelly trusted in Jesus Christ for the payment of her sin, so she would go to heaven one day. She and I had many talks and more than anything else on earth, she wanted all of her family and friends to be with her in heaven as well."

The pastor paused and looked over the several hundred people, before he pressed on. "If you are not yet trusting in the Lord Jesus, and you want to be with Kelly one day in heaven, stand up now and I will pray for you."

One young man who sat in the Amen pew sprang to his feet. Several minutes passed in silence before another stood up, and then another. Before long, all of the cheerleaders and soccer players stood up. As the people stood, cries with praise came to the lips of many... finally one last person stood to receive Jesus Christ... Kevin Bouman. One hundred people joined the pastor in prayer to receive Christ into their hearts... and then the contemporary Christian song play – My Father's Big Big House – played on. I could almost see Kelly's impish smile pass over so many who had loved her and that day came to a relationship with Jesus Christ. I thought, "Sometimes we must go into the night before we can see the Son rise."

CHAPTER 19
UNREST

I was aware of the deep canyon separating us and we found it impossible to climb over. No matter if we were getting along or not I no longer found Bill interesting or enjoyable. He loved everything I did not. We had nothing in common. He wanted to play church softball, I wanted to witness to the world that Christ had saved me. He enjoyed platitudes of silly stories, and I looked for the purpose Christ had for me and my family.

"What is it you want from me? I go to church with you. I bought you a house. You need nothing. But you are never ever satisfied," Bill said. "Can't you accept me for who I am?"

"And why can't you accept me for who I am?" I asked.

It was true, Bill was attending church, even went to Sunday school class, joined a men's bible study and was asked to be a deacon. But we were still not connected. I resented the church for asking Bill to serve in leadership when I saw that my husband continually had one foot in the world and the other in the Christ.

A question wrapped around my mind, one layer after another. Had I married the wrong man? In my sinful nature I married 'second best and not God's best' for me. That idea made me sad to think how much I had screwed up my life. Did I mess up the marital bliss that was intended for me because of my own stupidity?

One weekend Bill suggested I go along on a trip to Colorado for the auction. He hinted that it would be helpful for us to get away by ourselves.

Once we arrived, we settled in a beautiful chateau in a little ski town north of Denver. As we looked through the brochures of activities the resort had to offer, we agreed to take a snowmobile trip. We were eager to do an activity that was new to the both of us and didn't involve talking. We were all talked out, as far as I was concerned.

There were twelve snowmobiles in a line with motors off. We dutifully listened to a red-face man with blonde hair tell us to put on our helmets and gloves. "I want you green-horns to do what I do, and go where I go. Don't lag too far behind, or you'll get lost, and don't ride my tail either; someone could get hurt."

"All right are we ready to follow the leader," said our snowmobile guide. His eyes grazed over each one of his orange suited patrons. He cleared his throat and said with all seriousness, "Let me repeat myself – keep up with me; these Rocky Mountains will teach you cruel lessons about wildlife if you are caught out here without a guide. So keep your eyes on me. In about thirty minutes we will stop, and after I do a head count, those who are riding double can switch drivers. Now let's get started. Turn on those engines."

Bill turned on the motor, and I snuggled close to him with a strong squeeze. A familiar heaviness clung to my chest. Is he God's intended for me?

"I want to drive, too. We get to switch at the midway point, right?" I yelled over the roar of the motors. Bill nodded with a smile.

A line of a dozen or more snowmobiles slowly followed one another from the building that housed the resort's equipment. Our eyes were planted upon our leader as he swung his vehicle in a wide circle. Our trip began at a low speed. We dutifully followed the leader over hills, around tall pines, and carefully passed by a shore of frozen water. The blanket of snow glistened under the day's sun. Icicles hung gracefully on the arms of God's creation, while snow bunnies scurried quickly into the wood.

I wondered if Bill took notice of God's creation. Of course, the more I tried to help him see God's majesty, the more he dug in his heels. He was a man who hated change and the changes in me – he wanted no part of. It had been an endless spiritual tug of war and I was downright tired of it all. The more I looked at Bill, the more I saw our sharp differences. We weren't alike at all. He loved sports. I did not. He was stubborn. I was flexible. He was an organizer, and I was not much for keeping schedules. I loved to give, and he watched our every penny.

"Lord God, help me to see my husband as you see him," I prayed.

Our guide waved his hand, as if to motion us to keep up with his speed. We were going much faster than we ever intended to go.

Bill positioned our snowmobile as the caboose of the line. "Come on, Bill," I quietly fumed. I noticed the faster the others went, the more determined my husband was to remain at our steady speed. He rounded his corners ever so carefully. He stubbornly paced our motored sled by refusing the coercion of peer pressure.

"Bill, hurry up," I said. "We're falling behind." Suddenly, I laughed out loud, and kept laughing at the ridiculousness of our situation. We now couldn't see our group ahead.

"Bill, come on. We have to catch up."

"I am not going to kill us on our first snowmobile ride for anyone," Bill said.

By now I was getting a little irritated. Why is it that I'm always waiting on Bill? Our children are getting older, time is passing us by and we're going nowhere.

When we came up over another hill, there they sat, our group. Our leader shook his head, as we pulled our snowmobile to the end of his line, at our rightful place.

Bill turned the engine off; we dismounted our vehicle, and stretched our legs with a brisk walk. "Wow, look at that," he said.

"We're approximately 10,800 feet above sea level. Look to your left, and savoir the 'Continental Divide.' Yes sir, there's no better place to be," said our guide.

We stood momentarily spellbound as we saw the mighty mountains stretch high into the powder blue sky. Praise filled my chest as I thanked God for His power and all of His glorious creativity.

Once our respite was over, it was time to re-saddle our behinds onto our snowmobile. Bill jokingly bowed and swept his arm towards the driver's seat. "Be my guest," he said.

Positioning myself majestically on the seat, I put my gloved hands on the handlebars and turned to my husband and said, "All I want to know is, how do I brake?"

"Weren't you paying attention?" he asked. His face creased with worry.

"I've got it, Bill. Don't be such a worry wart." I quickly scanned over our snowmobile.

"Nikki, before you take off, listen to me," Bill said. He then recounted detailed instructions in how to brake and accelerate our machine. "And watch how you take your turns."

"Okay, okay," I said in exasperation.

One by one we moved out behind our guide. I was determined to keep up with the rest, no matter what the speed. My excitement kindled as I grasped the handlebars, turned up the throttle, and flew.

"Nikki!" Bill shouted. "Careful!"

The ride was great, but my passenger was a bit tense. "Slow down around the curves."

I took in the sights as we sped along the mountainside's trail. "Thank you, Lord, for the winter season with the beauty of the snow-capped mountains, and the gift of sight to appreciate them. And, Lord, I praise you for my husband."

Quietly, but ever so clearly, I heard from the Lord.

"Nikki, without you, Bill wouldn't go anywhere. But without Bill, you would fall off the side of the mountain."

For the next few moments, I pondered over the words God had said to me. The more I thought about it, the clearer His message became.

Bill and I were a perfect balance of personalities. He needed me to encourage him to trust God, to take risks in faith and to enjoy the ride of life. I needed Bill to keep me well grounded, to be my voice of reason, and to slow me down in my pursuit of life's adventures. My tendency to jump before I had all the information to make a good decision had been and still at times can be my demise.

The snowmobile ride was just what God ordered for our sickly marriage. I had a new appreciation for how God carefully and strategically put the two of us together. Our marriage is not second best – it is God's best. With that understanding, I knew the best was yet to come.

CHAPTER 20
BACK INTO THE FAMILY

After our Colorado weekend, I saw a change. Not necessarily in Bill but in me. I was no longer comparing Bill to others or to myself. I saw him as the perfect man for me and noted the differences between he and I were meant to be.

Bill grew ever so carefully in his faith. One day the auction's original owner named Art, died at an old age of 91. Our friend Greg had been witnessing to Art and hoped God changed his heart from an Unitarian to having a personal relationship with Jesus Christ. I too wrote Art and asked him to examine his faith against the holy scriptures. Bill connected well to Art but let us do the witnessing. We were surprised to hear that Art asked Bill and Greg to speak at his memorial service. The night before the service the Unitarian pastor called Bill and said, "I understand that you and Greg are Christians. I'm asking you to refrain from speaking about your beliefs in our church," she said. Bill's face turned a little red when he answered her and said, "Art knew exactly what we believed and I find it funny that he asked us to speak. You can not dictate to me what to say or not to say."

At the next's day service, my husband gave the best gospel presentation I had ever heard. My heart swelled with pride and I never again questioned where he was spiritually. Now that he is an elder in the church I can honestly stand by him as I have watched him stand by Christ.

One afternoon, three years after the separation from my mother and sisters, I received a phone call from Keitly.

"Nikki, mom's had a heart attack. You need to get to the hospital."

As I drove over to the hospital to see my mother, thoughts whirled around in my mind. Was she going to die? How would she receive me? How would the family react to me? I prayed, "Lord, please don't let her die without you. And please help my family to accept me."

The scripture that the Lord had given me a few years before all of this rose up to the forefront of my mind. *"No longer will violence be heard in your land, nor ruin or destruction within your borders, but you will call your walls*

Salvation and your gates Praise. The Sun will no more be your light by day nor will the brightness of the moon shine on you, for the Lord will be your everlasting light, and your God will be your glory. Your sun will never set again, and your moon will wane no more; The Lord will be your everlasting light, and your days of sorrow will end. Then will all your people be made righteous and they will possess the land forever. They are the shoots I have planted, the work of my hands, for the display of my splendor. The least of you will become a thousand, the smallest a mighty nation. I am the Lord; in its time I will do this swiftly." (Isaiah 60:18-22 NIV)

I entered the hospital with a new confidence. The first person I saw was Jody, who immediately came to my side. "Nikki, I'm glad you're here," she said with tears.

I walked into the room where my mother lay after her emergency bypass surgery. Was this the lady I sparred with so many times over the years? Was she the mother I craved for the affections I needed as a daughter but felt they were held in reserve. I looked to her eyes set upon her husband. Her eyes would follow his every move. I saw her complete dependence upon him. I came up alongside of her and said, "Mom I'm here."

Her complexion was ashen and her hair white, she looked at me and said, "I'm glad you're here. Please let's forget about all that has happened. We are family. We have the same blood."

I sat with mom that day and then over the next few weeks, I helped my mother when or where I could. I was happy that I was accepted back into the family. From then on, I concentrated on building up my relationships with my mom, step-father, sisters, and the rest of my blood family.

One summer day, while Meg was visiting her dad on the Cape and Stephanie visited a friend overnight, I said to Bill, "Why don't we get a hold of mom and see if she and my step-dad will want to share some hard shell crabs?"

"Go ahead and do that while I do an errand," he suggested.

At first the phone line was busy. I kept trying until finally my mother picked up. I heard her say, "Hello."

"Hi mom it's Nikki," I said.

The phone line crackled with interference, and then I heard the most frightening voice of evil say, *"Leave her alone!"*

A rush of adrenaline came up my spine. "No I will not! In the name of Jesus I rebuke you."

The line cleared and my mother said, "Nikki, are you there?" Incredibly my mother heard nothing but the static.

Nothing happened that day as we met and shared a meal together. I came to realize that my prayers and actions of love and acceptance were powerful tools of dismantling the enemy's control in my family members.

My growth in Christ continually challenged me in being a wife, mother, daughter, sister, or friend. I knew I would be tested at every corner and it was my choice to trust God and do things His way or not.

CHAPTER 21
HIS LIGHT ON OUR DARKNESS

As the years marched on, I prayed fervently for my children. "Lord, please grant them grace not to give the devil a foothold in their lives. Help them to make 'right' choices. And for some reason I always prayed that Meg would marry a pastor and Stephanie would marry a missionary.

Meagan grew into a beautiful person inside and out with standards in friendships and generally a hard worker in whatever she did. That didn't mean she didn't challenge us with teenage pursuits.

There was a day I had a phone call from Meg's supervisor at the local farm store/restaurant that employed her. The restaurant was good for her since she was allowed time off for her tennis season for matches or any extra-curricular activities.

"Hello, this is Elton from Oregon Diary. Is Meg there?"

"No, she should be home from school at any moment," I said.

"Is she sick?" he asked.

"No. Why do you ask?"

"Meagan called in about an hour or so ago and said she was sick. She won't be able to make it at 4:00 for her shift. I hate to question her but there is the biggest football game of the year at her school tonight. If she had asked me for time off a few days ago, there would have been no problem. Now it is a problem. So can you have her call me once she gets home?"

I sat on our sofa in the living room and watched Meg drive up in her little car. Her long dark hair hung below her shoulders. She bounded toward the front door with her report card in hand.

"Hey mom. Guess what? I made high honor roll this time," she said.

"Oh that's great. How are you feeling?" I asked. "Why don't you have a seat?"

"Really good," she said. "Why, what's wrong?" My kids always knew that the heart to heart talks were done in our living room.

"Meagan Shawn, do you remember how I pray for you?" I asked.

Meg sat down on the chair across from me. She crossed her legs and rested her chin in her hand.

"I pray that God will let his light shine on any darkness in your life. That He will expose it quickly. Did you call Elton this afternoon to tell him you were sick?" I asked.

I watched my daughter's long eyelashes cast to the floor. Her face was flushed and she said, "Mom, I just want to go to the football game. It's the biggest one of the year."

"I understand that. But you lied to Elton. He said he wants you to call him now. If you wanted off for the game you should have asked for it days earlier."

"Mom what shall I do? I don't want to talk to him."

"That's too bad. You do not have an option. Call him and apologize."

I went upstairs and heard my daughter dial the phone. I heard her low tone of voice and I carefully picked up the extension to make sure she was really talking with Elton.

I only heard Elton say, "You're fired."

I quietly put the receiver back down and waited for my daughter to come to me with tears. Instead she came to me with more questions. "Mom, Elton said if I am not at work within the next few minutes I'm fired. What shall I do? I don't want to get fired but I want to go to the football game."

"I can't make that decision for you. You need to figure this one out for yourself. There are consequences to all of our choices."

My stomach rolled as I watched her struggle. She quickly put on her waitress outfit and ran out the door.

That night when she came home I asked her how work went.

"Elton pulled me into his office once I got there and he said that the whole kitchen staff had bets that I wouldn't show up for work."

"Oh, really?"

"Elton said he knew I be at work because he told me that I'm a girl that has integrity and character."

I realized how the Lord works with our children. We can train up ou r children in the way they should go but God is the one who never lets His word fall to the ground. When we allow Him to do His work with conviction and consequences our children are rewarded with their own faith walk. God has answered my prayers - both of my daughters married men of faith. Meagan married a pastor.

CHAPTER 22
BRING THEM INTO YOUR OWN HOMES

When Meg went off to college in the next couple of years we had built an extension on our home with another bathroom and bedroom. A friend of mine who was in a ministry with international students asked me if I would take a young Korean girl into our home. After prayer and discussion with family members, we decided it might be fun for Stephanie to have someone a little older than she, from a different culture, living with us for the school year. Her name was Hyun Jin Rim.

Jin was a beautiful girl of 14 years old. She had the maturity level of one much older. Jin came from a Christian family but was not yet one who believed. She watched us have family devotions, pray, and worship together.

Jin was polite and fun. We would play Uno with her to communicate with numbers. At least they were universal.

Over the year I would pray, "How can we reach her for you Lord?" Jin would laugh at us when we prayed or did family devotions. She couldn't understand the reasoning behind church for more that once a week. She was a typical teenager who had no relationship with Christ.

After a year of watching and waiting for the Lord to work in Jin's life He opened a door wide through our long summer drought of that year. Little did I know at the time that God would orchestrate something so simple but unusual that would grant light to Jin's eyes.

Almond eyes question
Quiet and reflective
Never sharing, hardly caring
Life is boring, no longer touring
Fifteen and seeking
For what all the creator offers
Prayerfully bypassing scoffers
Seek and ye shall find
Contentment in His perfection
One day I'll see His reflection
In those beautiful almond eyes

Pennsylvania had a drought this particular summer and our area was put on restriction. We were told how much water we could use and how and when we could use the water. Our water meter was checked every week and if our house had gone over the limit we were to pay a fine of six hundred dollars. I heard rumors of several in our neighborhood that received a fine. I was surprised that the drought lasted so long and the water level wasn't up to what it needed to be, even late into the fall.

One October morning, Pastor John called and asked, "Nikki there is an old-order Mennonite woman with six children that needs our help. Her husband is in jail for abuse. Apparently, the woman decided to leave him and he went after her with his truck. Pushed her vehicle off the road and she got out of her driver's seat to try to calm him down. While the children sat inside their mom's van, the watched their daddy put his hands around her neck to strangle her. Thank God for a good Samaritan who came upon the scene and called the police. This fellow pulled the husband off of his wife. Now that her husband is sitting in jail she needs to get out of there. The police told her to leave her home now and go into hiding. And by the way, she is several months pregnant too."

Six kids and one on the way, wow, I thought.

"Do you think that you and Bill can help her pack up the house? She doesn't have much but she needs to get out of that house. We are working on a place for her to go but it's going to be a couple of days."

"Bill's out of town until Thursday. I'll call Lori and her husband and see if they will help.

Stephanie, Jin and I drove over to the address that Pastor John had given. The gray crooked house sat wearily along side of the road. There was a barn at its right a few feet away.

We pulled into the dirt driveway and went to the door. The door window had a yellowed shade drawn over a large crack. "Who's there?" a young girl asked.

"Hi, we were asked by our church to come and help your mother out. Can we come in?" I asked.

The little girl with one leg opened the door. "Hi, I'm Anna. I'm nine years old and I'm home schooled." She grinned. Stephanie reached out her hand and said, "I'm twelve and I go to Living Word Academy."

Twin baby boys were toddling from one room to another. The boys were dressed shabbily. Another boy ran into the kitchen where we were standing. "Mom's coming. She's packing right now. My name is Jeremy, what's yours?"

Jin smiled shyly and said, "Hyun Jin Rim. I'm from Korea."

"Wow that's on the other side of the world isn't it?" Anna said.

"Yes it is. It's chilly in here. Don't you guys have heat?" I asked.

"Daddy broke the thermostat," said Jeremy.

Jeremy was a little older than Anna and I could tell he was trying to be the man of the house.

"We are here to help your mama pack. Where is she?"

Jeremy went to the stairs and shouted, "Mom, company. People from a church are here to help us."

Anna showing Stephanie and Jin her missing leg. "I was born like this but I can get around pretty good. I can even climb up to the loft in the barn. That's where we hide from daddy when he's mad."

A woman carrying a box came into the kitchen where we were standing. She had her black hair pulled back into a bun. Strands of gray fell down over her left cheek. Round gray eyes with large black bags marked her thin face. "I don't really have that much to pack."

"Hi my name is Nikki. Show us what we can do."

"I'm Sara. We are appreciative of the help."

Sara then showed us into the living room area. "I only want our books. He can have the chair and table. I'll take the couch. Pack up our kitchen. Leave him some things so he has something to eat off or to cook in." Two other children raced through the kitchen and came to their mother's side. "Mama, we're done packing our room."

"Ok girls. Go on outside and play."

The twin boys lay on the couch, listless and cold. "Is it their nap time?" I asked.

"They're not feeling good. Both have a fever."

"Can we get them some blankets? It's so cold in here," Lori asked.

Sara went to a closet and pulled out a threadbare blanket. "They can share."

Lori and Dick came over with a truck the church rented for the move. "Hi guys. I'm so glad you're here. This packing shouldn't take too long. Man it's freezing in here. It's October but it feels like January," I said.

We worked all that morning and into to the afternoon. "Listen, we'll be back to help you after dinner.

The kids and I went home to eat. "I think that we should bring some blankets to the family tonight. It's going down into the teens tonight."

"Mom, shouldn't we let them come into our house for the night. That's what I think real Christians would do," Stephanie suggested.

Jin looked at me with her almond shaped eyes and waited for my response. "You know what, I think you're right. Dad's not home and we have the room. Will you two sleep together?"

"Yes. Sure," Stephanie said and Jin gave a nod. Jin talked in fragments of English. "I want to, er, eh, how you say… ?" She motioned with her hands as if she were bathing a dog. "Oh, you want to give the children a bath?" I asked. "Sure, we can do that."

I did think of our water shortage and all those children. Lord, help me. I don't want to get fined.

After we returned to the house, Lori and Dick too were there. I asked Sara if she would care to come to my home and be warm for the night. She agreed and asked if she could take a warm shower at the house. "Can you take my farm hands with us?" Sara asked. Dick and Lori immediately offered the two men a basement room to stay in.

That night all the children had a bath; they were so dirty that we had to empty the tub each time before another child could climb in. Sara had a long hot shower and all the children had clean warm pajamas to climb into. Three children climbed into Steph's bed and the twin babies slept in Meg's room with their mama. Jeremy, the oldest, slept next to mom on the carpeted floor cushioned with several blankets.

"Bill, I'm sorry. I thought this was the best thing to do. Their thermostat was broken and it's so cold tonight."

"They must be gone by the time I get home. This is crazy Nikki. You're bringing strangers into our home? What happens if her husband gets out and comes after her?"

"The police have him for another twenty four hours. That should be enough time for the church to get her out of their home. Besides, Lori and Dick also brought the two farmhands into their home for overnight," I said.

"This is nuts," Bill said.

That night Sara and her children had a comfortable warm bed to sleep in and the next morning I gave them a good breakfast. A couple from our church drove the moving truck and the family to a place in Massachusetts that would help her get settled.

The amazing part of the story is that the drought restrictions were lifted that very day. And Jin's eyes were opened to Christianity.

CHAPTER 23
WITNESS

"Lord I try to teach my children to tell others about You, but what kind of example am I? I can't seem to get beyond my Jerusalem. Please open a door of opportunity and when You answer this prayer, please supply enough grace for me to speak up for you, amen," I prayed.

It was a rainy Monday. "Perfect," I said with satisfaction. I love to take care of our home on Mondays, so it might as well rain.

As the day went on, tasks of dusting, scrubbing floors and toilets, had my full attention. No longer did I think on my earlier conversation with the Lord.

"Mom, there's a man at the door. You'd better answer it," Stephanie said.

I was in the middle of laundry and needed to prepare dinner. "Ugh, what does he want? Too many solicitors and they try my patience," I grumbled.

As I opened the door a young man with a black knit cap, oversized army jacket, and identification badge stood before me in the rain.

"Can I help you?" I asked.

"Hi. My name is Chris Brown. Last year you donated to help our organization, the Pennsylvania Federation of Sportsmen Clubs. Do you remember?"

"No. Not really," I said quietly.

Chris began listing all of the ways that PFSC had provided funds for cleaning up parks and creating bike paths.

Chris had tension written all over his face.

"Hey, come in. Get out of the rain at least. I'll write you a check for a donation. It won't be much but it's better than nothing."

Chris eyes lit up. "Thanks."

While I wrote a check out for ten dollars I sought ways to make conversation. "I can give you an umbrella if you need it and if I can find one. We have a knack of leaving them wherever we go."

Chris smiled. "I'm alright. Thanks for your contribution and here's a receipt."

We said goodbye and off I headed for the laundry room.

As I pulled clothes from the dryer, I suddenly felt conviction. "Did you want me to share the good news with Chris Brown?"

"Lord, I'm sorry," I prayed. "Please forgive me and help me to do better next time."

I delivered the clean clothing to the right bedrooms and headed for the kitchen when the doorbell rang.

I opened the door and there stood Chris Brown.

"Chris what do you need?" I asked. Chris looked confused and stunned. He stuttered out an apology and said, "I must have lost my sense of direction."

My heart jumped into my throat. I didn't open my mouth. I watched him walk away in the rain. No words would come. "Lord, please help me."

"Chris," I yelled. He stood at the top of my driveway.

"Yes, ma'am?" he turned.

"Do you know Jesus?"

"Er, yes, ma'am, I do," he slowly returned to my front door. "I mean I used to go to church but I haven't been for a long time."

"Jesus Christ loves you. He sent you back to me so that I could tell you. He has changed my life dramatically and wants to do the same for you."

Chris' eyes searched my face. He was silent for a moment. "Thank you, ma'am."

"Thank Him," I suggested.

Warmed by God's presence, I slowly closed the door. I turned toward my kitchen and ran into Stephanie. My child's eyes were filled with love and admiration.

"Remember this is what we are called to do. We are to tell others about Jesus' love so they too may come out of the rain."

CHAPTER 24
MY PLACE IN HIS CHURCH

My prayer life began to change as I grew in Christ. I found I was no longer praying for comfort and the family's salvation. I began thanking God for His promises that He would make everyone in my land righteous by the work of His hand and in His time He would do it swiftly. Now I concerned myself in being used by God to do whatever it was He wanted to do.

"Lord, I have nothing to offer you except the use of my hands, feet, and mouth. Show me what it is you desire to do through me," I prayed.

I sought the Lord fervently for several months. I had this incredible stirring within my spirit that would not rest.

I knew I was to serve Jesus in His church but I really wasn't cut out for nursery. It seemed to me that it was the only thing I could do. "Lord, please show me the way. Do you want me to serve in the nursery? Shall I help out in the kitchen for Vacation Bible School?"

I did do those things but I was not at all comfortable. In the nursery I felt as if it were a real chore and for the kitchen work I was admonished by one woman when she said, "Go somewhere else. I'll do the cookie display. This is not where you need to be." I was insulted at first. Later, I recognized that it was the Lord's voice directing me out of the places He did not call me to do.

One day as I was reading James 2, I suddenly knew what it was the Lord wanted from me.

The Church is a wealthy body of believers. Caucasian, white-collar professionals with an abundant amount of gifts in education, talents and money are the members of the 600 congregation. This church is faithful in preaching and teaching God's word in spirit and truth from the pulpit to the Sunday school classes. They give 33 percent to mission-aries called to serve in several countries around the world. Yet there was something missing. Those who did not have the gift of teaching or the gifts that go along with that had nowhere to serve...

What good is it my brothers, if a man claims to have faith but has no deeds? Can such faith save him? Suppose a brother or sister is without clothes and daily food. If one of you says to him, "Go, I wish you well; keep warm and well fed," but does nothing about his physical needs, what good is it? In the same way, faith by itself, if it is not accompanied by action, is dead.

I understood. I could see. Westminster needed to feed and clothe. Our church needed a food and clothing bank. There began a two-year battle of obtaining the session's approval through a committee formed as the Salt & Light committee. I was told to research and present the facts to the committee. I sought out others who had gone on before me in other churches who had started these things. The initial reaction to my presentation was negative. I would hear it from other members in the congregation. "We don't want to become a social church," several members said. Others said, "Right. A food and clothing bank within a church like ours… for what purpose? Who is going to use it?"

Eyes were blinded and not opened to the fact that several families were experiencing a loss of a job or an illness. Those naysayers could not see the burdens of the lost around us. I saw the potential for evangelism purposes.

I was given the approval for a clothing give away within a year. My first clothing drive was intended to clothe those in our church who were hurting and to invite the public to come in and participate in our table. I felt strongly that the clothes were given with the gospel by using a tract. I remember another organization outside of our church thought that this was tasteless and obnoxious.

"Why do you say such a thing?" I asked. "How are they going to know the reason for our generosity? We cannot pretend it is for any other reason other than that Christ loves them."

I found in the Proverbs the scripture that says, "A gift provides the way for the giver." God provides the way through His spirit and our gifts.

That first clothing drive was quite interesting. I had a small committee of women who had the same desire to be a part of this ministry. We advertised in our bulletin, "Give only what you would want to receive." In other words don't give us your trash, only clean clothes in excellent order.

The entire one side of our large activity room was filled with clothes. The small group of women separated, folded and placed on tables according to gender and age. I had made flyers and contacted the news media for the big morning. It was a lot of hard work but we were ready for the crowds we were sure would attend.

Exactly 12 people came. They were families from our church that were in need. There wasn't one person that attended that came from the 'outside.' I fussed and asked God, "Why? What is it you want me to do?"

His Spirit pressed me to go and look into the yellow pages for shelters. Here were a few listed but one responded. It was Clare House on Chestnut Street. "Yes, there are five women here and we will love to come to your clothing give-away. But we need a ride."

So there it began. After the women feasted on the rich excellent clothes for themselves and their children we were asked, "Will you pick us up to go to your church tomorrow?"

The women were a training ground for me and an instrument of the Lord's to teach me. There was a woman named Janie who was quiet and unassuming. She had an unmanageable toddler boy who ruled his mother. Janie told us that her husband was in prison for selling drugs and was waiting for his sentence to end.

I tried to come up alongside of Janie and the others and wanted to help them in any way. The other members of our church too reached out. A friend of mine named Donna would gladly pick up Janie and take her in town to look for an apartment or take her to the drug store to get a prescription filled.

One day, we read that Janie was arrested for trying to buy heroine. Now it made sense to all of us that Janie used Donna and the others to pick up not Tupperware or prescriptions but hits of heroine. We were aghast. Janie was a liar to the ninth degree and we needed to learn how to be street savvy if we were to be a part of God's outreach team.

But through the invitation to the clothing give away and the rides to church the women begged us to come in to Clare House on Thursdays and give us a Bible Study. They had a mandatory Bible Study each week for one hour on Thursday and the older woman in their opinion was 'boring' so we were asked.

Donna and I took the helm and were delighted to share the gospel of Jesus Christ. We didn't have a clue what we were doing but we tried to be faithful to the scriptures. I remember in the beginning we tended to lean too much on our experiences. It was then the Lord admonished me to keep it all about Jesus Christ.

Within four years of that ministry we spent every Thursday night at Bible Study in Clare house to a small group of homeless women who were allowed to live there for three months before they were helped to find a job and an apartment. The women were given classes on parenting and had to pursue their GED or classes to hone in skills for the work force. I saw many women move in and out. Donna and I would help them with food, items for homemaking such as any kitchenware and anything that was sent to us to give.

One Thursday we met a young woman who was chic in looks. She was black with short-cropped hair and wore a bandana around her head. Karen Smith attended our study in attitude. She was quiet and annoyed that she was made to attend these studies. She would come in at the last moment of time before we started and was the first to rush out the door.

The other women opened up and shared their prayer requests but not Karen. One Thursday, Donna and I made are normal entrance to a household of crying females.

"What in the world is going on?" I asked.

"They came and took her. She's in prison now," another young black woman cried.

"Tiff, what do you mean? Who are they and who did they take?" I asked.

"The police took Karen. Karen Smith," Tiffany said with black mascara under her eyes.

Another one of the girls name Josie said, "Yeah she was out on bail waiting for her trial here. Karen was busted three months ago. She thought she wouldn't have to serve but she was wrong. She was here trying to get her life back and make enough money to get her an apartment and get her kids back."

"Where are her kids?" I asked.

"Children and Youth Services have them. And that's a bitch getting your children out of the system," a tall woman named BJ said.

Tiffany said, "Write her. Help her."

"Karen didn't like us too much," Donna said. "Are you sure she wants a letter from either one of us?"

Tiffany looked at me. "Write her. Please write her."

So I wrote Karen. I wrote her a short note to Lancaster County Prison.

Dear Karen,

Why didn't you tell us what was happening with you?
We would have prayed for you and your children.
If there is anything we can do for you, let us know.
Remember Jesus loves you...Nikki

That was the beginning of many letters written to Karen and Karen writing back. I understood that I was the only one writing her at the time. All of her friends and family refused to communicate with her. Karen did write her children and they wrote her back yet they were young.

When I wrote Karen, I would ask her questions about the meaning of certain scriptures. I sent her a bible and asked her to look up the verses and answer me. She at first ignored my requests but she knew that in order to keep our communication open she had to answer my questions.

Dear Nikki,   *3-22-95*

I received your letter last night and this morning I started a lesson in a bible study. The study was on "The Joy of Forgiveness." God is really working on me. The lesson states that guilt feelings can block the way to experience the joy of forgiveness. The scriptures in 1 John and Romans 8 that you gave to me to read, were the very same I had in my lessons this morning. I pray for God to help me and guide me in the right direction and He sends your letters to me. I ask for his help to understand the Bible and he sits me in the company of roommates who love and believe in Him. I see His work all around me, every day.

Our first visit to Muncie State Prison where Karen had been transferred, Donna and I had a road trip of confusion. We seemed to take lefts instead of rights and generally weaved our way through a maze of confusion. Once we got to the prison Donna walked through security metal alarm system and beeped. "Do you have any keys in your pocket or are you wearing any jewelry?" the gruff officer asked.

Donna was nervous to begin with and her face and mind went blank. "No."

"Walk through again," he said.

I stood aside and encouraged Donna to go ahead.

The alarm went off again and then again. Donna paled a bit and said, "Honest officer I have nothing on me."

I watched my friend squirm. Donna's comedic personality had me laughing yet the joke was at its end with another beep.

"You're not going to strip search me are you?" Donna asked.

Suddenly, I knew what was going on. "Excuse me officer, my friend has a metal plate in her right leg which she shattered this past winter. Would that cause the beeps?" I asked.

The officer nodded and Donna sighed with relief. As we walked out of the guard's house and into the designated area to meet Karen, Donna fussed about the guard's attitude. "Do I look like a criminal? Honest to Pete I thought he was going to make me take my clothes off."

Once we made our way into the large visitation room we waited for Karen's arrival.

Karen was ushered through a metal door and to our table. A bright white smile gleamed as she approached us. "Nikki," she hugged Donna, "Thank you for coming."

I laughed out loud. "Do all white people look alike to you? I'm Nikki."

She laughed with embarrassment, then sat us down to tell us a story what had happened to her the evening before.

"You won't believe what happened to me. Maybe you can tell me what it means." She looked to me and then to Donna.

"Go ahead, we're all ears, that we're here," Donna said. Donna was still recovering from the metal detector experience.

"I was lying on my cot and my cellie was sleeping. I heard the Hispanic women playing craps down the hall. I was trying to sleep but couldn't. Suddenly I felt a huge hand on my back and I heard a man's voice say, "Karen you can't go back.""

Karen's large dark eyes widened with fright. "I don't know what that was all about but it scared the pants off of me."

"Karen, now that you're a Christian, God is just telling you that you can't go back to your old way of life," I said.

"Wow. That's right. That's what He's saying to me," Karen said. "There's nothing to go back to anyway. Hey, Dr. Rogers (our church's pastor) wrote to me. I sent him a letter with some of my cartoon characters I drew."

"That's one of your talents for certain; drawing," I said.

"It's time to write me now," Donna said.

"Sure. I will. I love to write."

Karen did love to write. She not only wrote me several times a week, she wrote Donna, Dr. Rogers, and two or three other women from our congregation in Westminster.

Karen wrote a poem to me around the same time she had asked Christ into her life...

One day
> *I decided that I didn't want to worry*
myself into an early grave
One day,
> *I decided that God is big enough*

And smart enough

    To handle my worries

One day

    I decided I would quit worrying

Have faith in God

    And trust God to protect me.

One day

    I decided I would quit worrying

About a release and

    Be released (freed) from the

Burden of sin within me

One day

    I decided to pray more and worry less

To talk to God about each and everything

    That's going on in my life

For He alone can free me

    Free me from this prison within

(And Muncy)

    That's when God's spirit touched me

And I realized that prayer

    Can change the outcome…Karen Smith

Near to the time that Karen was to be released, we worked hard in getting her a place of residence. First she was required to go back to the Clare House for three months. Bill lined up a job at the Auction for Karen, and we began to meet the requirements listed from the state to get Karen's children out of foster care.

The Pastor warned her that our church was 99 percent white. She wrote back and said, "It doesn't bother me. These are my people now."

The day she was released, Donna picked her up at the bus station. She drove her directly to the church in her prison uniform with two pigtails on either side of her head.

After our hugs and kisses, Karen and Donna walked into the church to meet the Pastor. There he walked at the end of the hall. Karen's tears poured down her cheeks as she ran down the hall calling his name with her arms out for a hug. Our Pastor opened his arms as Karen put her head into his chest sobbing. He quietly spoke into her ear, "It's ok Karen. You're free now. You're home now."

The white church produced an apartment to rent with their signature on the lease, donated furniture and other necessities such as a washer/dryer, television, appliances - all that is needed for a home to function properly. With the evidence of a job and help with the prison fees, Karen was able to get her children out of foster care. Now she had her ten-year-old son and five-year-old daughter home with her.

But that's not the end of Karen's story. Karen had been diagnosed in prison with sarcoidosis, which is a lung disease that could be and was in fact fatal to Karen. She died six years later. The church and all those in Karen's life cared for Karen and her children when she couldn't work after the first year of being out of prison; car fumes were terribly damaging to her lungs. Karen collected disability and had help from her church, her people, for the rent of her low income apartment. Karen and her family were blessed over and over again from the food and clothing banks that the church supplied. Lori and Dick opened their home to Karen's boy for more than a year, and then he went on to live with his sister's family. Karen's little girl lived with a family who loved her as their own.

At Karen's funeral I told her story and gave God the glory at all that he had done. We knew that God's amazing grace brought many people to Christ through Karen's testimony. She fought her demons and overcame the obstacles of disease to glorify Christ in all she did for the rest of her life here on earth.

I introduced Karen to my family before she died. I told them her story and they were impressed that she lived her life well after "going to church." I find it funny that I had to walk through my own father's imprisonment in order to reach out to one that was imprisoned. Or I had to experience the drug life to know a bit of the life that my friend Karen trusted in. I was and am able to relate but it isn't about me. It is Christ in me, and his use of my brokenness to help others.

CHAPTER 25
OUTSIDE OF MY JERUSALEM

B ill, Stephanie and I were invited to go on a mission's trip to Kingston, Jamaica. Actually, we as the adults were to help chaperone ten college students.

I was forty years old and had never been on a mission's trip and I was scared to death of what lay ahead. Sandy Good, a member of our church, a mission professor at Lancaster Bible College invited Bill, I, and our 10-year-old daughter to minister the gospel with a group of his college students. Thankfully he brought his wife Diane, a friend of mine, and their 14-year-old daughter, Marsha, with her best friend, Elisa.

Our flight was short and without incident. We were entering another country so it was another first for me. After landing and walking through the busy and poorly organized airport, we could see the stress on Sandy's face. Bill was used to keep track of all pieces of luggage and passports.

I was at once aware of the contrast of beauty versus a harsh reality of poverty. As we drove on the narrow winding streets to our home for ten days, I took note of the green mountainous terrain against the deep blue skies. I was astonished at the cows walking without evidence of any owner, ducking their heads into the gullies filled with trash to fill their skeletal frame. Goats, pigs and chickens too were everywhere on the road slipping in and out of the fast moving traffic. Several shanties lined the mountain's side and other windowless huts obviously were places of business in sales of fruit or meat that sat sleepily at the street's edge. Tin roofed shanties with no windows were the home to many of the poor. I wondered what it was like when strong gales of winds blew through this area. How were the people protected against the storms? As our van climbed the mountain surrounding Kingston, I took note of rich homes surrounded by high walls and locked gates that looked down upon the poverty-stricken below. I wondered if I were one who lived below with the poor, would I harbor anger and resentment, every time I looked upward.

We arrived at the house with five or six bedrooms, a large living room with high ceilings and wood floors. Sliding glass doors opened onto a veranda where we were blessed to watch hummingbirds feed at the morning's dawn. A large built in pool sat to the left of the house for our afternoon pleasure of cooling off from the Jamaican sun. Our family along with the girls and the older couple stayed at a home, not too far from the main house. Our meetings and meals were always at the main house with the rest of the team.

Sandy had our team go door to door in evangelism during the day, and held meetings at night under a streetlight in the worst neighborhoods of Kingston. I was immediately intimidated. I knew that I could not for the life of me do any good to any one without God's help.

The arranged skits, testimonies, songs of grace from those who were musical, and Sandy's preaching were a blessing to the crowds. Bill also preached two sermons while we were there.

One night as I was to give my testimony, I began to share what God had done in my life, and the crowds became loud and riotous. Police with a machine gun in a jeep made its rounds through the mob of people before me. I kept going even though I didn't see the Lord at work. Once I finished, two Mormon elders on bicycles came over to me to tell me that they enjoyed my testimony. Even in chaos God is at work.

I enjoyed the Jamaican people in their honesty. When we went door-to-door evangelism I would ask if the person was a Christian. "No. Not yet. Later when I am old I will ask Jesus into my heart."

One woman laughed when I asked her if she had a personal relationship with Christ. "You can't know God personally," she howled.

Others would listen and ask questions and even pray the prayer to receive Christ. Meanwhile, there was one young man on our team who was extremely sick the entire time we were in Kingston. He became our prayer warrior. One who could never go out but interceded for each and every one of us.

One afternoon Bill and I were walking through a depressed area of Kingston, when I saw two young women strolling down the dirt lane. They were dressed in short skirts, low cut blouses and had lots of jewelry on.

I looked over at them and said to Bill, "They won't listen to us. Do you want to give them a tract?"

"Might as well. It's been slow this afternoon. We haven't talked to anyone but the laughing woman."

"OK, here goes," I said.

"Hello. Do you know Jesus?" I asked. "Would you like to know Jesus?"

One of the women raised her arms toward heaven with tears pouring down her face. "Yes I want to know Jesus. I don't want to live this kind of life anymore. Tell me how to become a Christian."

God showed me in a great way that day that I cannot judge; only He knows the heart of a human being.

I'll never forget my first trip out of my comfort zone. It was filled with intense warfare, many converts, great testimonies and a lesson on judging the hearts.

CHAPTER 26
FEAR NOT

"These here gators love marshmallows," said our guide as he gruffly presented the plastic bag before us. "Now take some and feed them."

I leaned over to Bill and whispered, "He could have cleaned up a bit don't you think?"

Bill gave me one of his funny grins. We giggled as we looked at our guides' greasy ball cap, an unkempt beard and ragged jeans. Bill spoke into my ear, "He could have the lead role in the movie Deliverance." For some reason I didn't find humor in my husband's observation. I was glad the waters were calm.

Two flat-bottomed boats carried the company's twenty yuppie patrons into the marshes of Louisiana. We were together on a business convention and chose to explore the Bayou on our free time.

When we came to a fork in the water the two boats parted. The absence of the other boat bothered me. I became uneasy. "Why didn't we go on the other boat?" I asked Bill. "At least their guide looked semi-professional."

The neck of the waters became increasingly narrow as dreary shadows camouflaged its riverbed. Our boat slowed and crept into a dark brush. "This is too scary," I said.

"Ya'll see those cypress trees?" our guide asked as he pointed a dirty finger. "The moss ya see hanging from them ther trees is where many a snake hides out." His smirk revealed a toothless smile. "Yeah, they do at times drop into the boat, but don't be alarmed cuz these here moccasins ain't poisonous."

A young man who sat directly across from me paled and spoke in a low but audible voice. "I hope that won't happen – I hate snakes."

The guide immediately lunged into a story. "Yeah there was a man a few weeks back who had such a fear of snakes that when one fell into the boat he jumped right into the water with the alligators."

Suddenly, it was impossible for me to gather enough spit to swallow. I was stiff with fear while I prayed, "Lord, help me. You know how much I hate snakes."

As our boat moved slowly away from shore, the guide explained to his captive audience about the many creatures that lived in the Bayou. Unfortunately, I heard only the words alligator, muskrat and snake. My eyes were busy scanning every tree with moss in it.

As we passed fishing campsites and shanties lined on the banks of the swamp, I wondered about the people who chose to live in them. "Who in their right mind would a want to live here?" I asked Bill. His shoulders shrugged and looked across the river to the green levy with wooden docks sprinkled about.

"It's a beautiful land. Think about the good this particular part of the country has to offer," Bill suggested.

Cajun food, trumpet players, storytellers and a brilliant history of southern hospitality were a few things that came to mind. The natural beauty of the Bayou is something all southern people are proud to display.

Before long we came to a basin of water where the guide shut the motor off. Our guide instructed us to wait quietly for few minutes as we dutifully threw marshmallows into the water.

It wasn't too long before alligator snouts lifted from water's current to snap up their treats. "These gators ya'll see here are the yonuns. See how small they are? The older ones are watching from the underbrush. We've seen a grand-daddy that's at least 8' long in these parts. Of course the gators are meat eaters. They feed mostly on other reptiles and mammals. And they do attack humans."

After a few moments with several teenage alligators, our guide re-started the boat's motor and we continued the tour. The boat rounded a corner and we came into a small-enclosed area. Many kinds of trees, flowers, and wildlife commanded our attention but all I was concerned about were the hanging snakes and hungry, watching alligators.

Twisted vines wrapped casually around each tree trunk stood on the marshy riverbed, suddenly came to life in my mind's eye. These woody vines suddenly had become weary snakes ready to drop into our drifting boat.

My imagination exploded as I pictured our guide telling 'my story' to his next group of tourists.

'On my last trip out a moccasin fell out of a tree and landed squarely on this hysterical woman. He was only 5' long- considered to be small in these here parts. I tried to tell her he wasn't going to do her any harm, but she wouldn't listen to me. She jumped and tripped over her own two feet

and she ended up with the granddaddy alligator of them all. That woman done panicked and drowned.'

"Nikki, are you all right? You look a little pale," Bill said.

"I'm fine," I lied.

"God please help me – I'm out of control," I prayed.

Scripture flashed to the forefront of my mind. *"Cast down your imagination. Fear not for I am with you.'*

"Okay, Lord. Thank you for reminding me of your word. By your grace I will fear no snake, alligator, or muskrat or even this scary looking guide. I'm sorry I haven't trusted you in the Bayou. Please forgive me and help me to enjoy the rest of this hour."

God gave me His peace and through new eyes I could see the beauty of God's creation in the Bayou. I saw the guide's love for the swampland and understood; God too, had created him. God loved him.

Once our group returned, we said our goodbyes to the guide and waited for the others to enter our tour bus. Thirty minutes passed before we finally saw the other flat-bottomed boat drift slowly back to their dock. Faces on the boat looked strained and weary. We gave a shout as they boarded and made their way to the back of the bus. "Did you get lost in the brush? What took you so long?" someone asked.

As their story unfolded I could feel the hairs on my arms stand up once more.

Their guide took a small detour to recover a six-foot moccasin that sunned itself on a dock of a shanty. He maneuvered the boat close to the dock, reached over, and pulled the snake onto the boat with his bare hands. He wanted to show his guests how harmless these snakes were but his plan backfired as the moccasin fought back. The guide ended up with a boat full of hysterical tourists. Horrified tourists watched their guide wrestle the snake until he pulled out his revolver and put a bullet into its head.

Breaths of relief lifted from my chest as I sat securely on my seat in the bus. God was gracious and kind enough to place Bill and me with *the* perfect tour guide and place *our* home far from the Bayou.

CHAPTER 27
MY FATHER'S HOUSE

For years my father lived far from me. He would call occasionally to ridicule me in my new life, yet for the most part I kept to myself. I didn't call him. I prayed for him, but kept away. Now I had to face him - he was dying in a Veteran's hospital in Vermont. He had asked to see his four daughters. Keitly and I drove together since my other two sisters were highly uncomfortable in my presence and made sure that they went to visit him earlier in the week. Keitly, although we were different in our Christian walks, we still had more in common. We drove together for several hours with nervous anticipation and tried to be calmer once we pulled into the parking lot of the hospital. We walked a long quiet hall to a nurses' station and asked what room he was in.

Once we entered the room, we saw an old man sleeping with a feathered shabby white beard which hung over a sunken torso. "Is that him?" I asked. "He looks so small."

Keitly's eyes moistened as she scanned his face. "Dad, Nikki and I are here."

"Well, hello there." Bloodshot green eyes danced as his ornery grin spread across his aged face. "If I knew my girls would visit me on my deathbed, I would have tried to die a long time ago."

I shot a glance at Keitly before I cleared my throat and said, "Dad, we're here now." The sterile room was large and had single beds lined down each side of the room. There were no curtains or petitions used for privacy.

"Dad, tell us what's going on with you? Are they able to help you here?" Keit's eyes shifted over to the nurse attending a wheezing patient.

"I'll know after my surgery tonight."

"Hey, you look good for an old broad, Nikki." His wink and remark pierced through me. My father's eyes rested on my face with a tinge of admiration. "You've done well for yourself. Or should I say, Bill has done well for you? You dress like the rich bitches I see in the city. What kind of car are you driving now?"

"A Volvo; and, yes, we're okay financially. If that's what you're asking."

Dad's shoulders raised and his voice deepened when he said, "Yeah, that's what I'm asking," His eyes shifted back to my sister and asked. "And what's this I hear you married again?"

"Yep. You'd like this one dad, he's a good guy," Keitly said.

His face softened and he closed his eyes. "Yeah, I probably would."

An inward breath raised his chest and then fell again with his exhale. "I need to get my house in order. I have a wife and kids who need taking care of."

Hmmm, I thought 'Dad's acting responsible – what a surprise.'

"What do you want done?" Keitly asked.

"Oh it's already in the works. I've made sure my Veteran's disability checks are signed over to Eileen. I've asked friends to watch over her and Jake. Jake's just 16 years old, still a pup; his brother Devon better step up to the plate to take care of his mother now that he's twenty-one."

"Dad, let us help you put your house in order - your spiritual house," I said.

A look of defiance and agitation crawled over my father's face. "Nikki, I had a conversation with Jesus before you got here. He told me to tell you to shut the f— up. He and I are okay."

Indignation and shock ran through my veins. "Dad, I don't believe that - not for one moment."

"Leave him alone, Nikki, maybe he is ok with Jesus," Keitly said.

I looked over at my youngest sister in disbelief. How could she think that dad had any kind of relationship with Jesus Christ when throughout our life he said the Bible was fabricated campfire stories passed on through the generations? I shot an angry glance at her.

"I'll be quiet for now, but before I leave this state I want you to listen to me. I want you to hear me out – so I can rest."

"Why should I listen to you when I'm a whole lot smarter than you are?" said Dad.

I met his eyes with a raised eyebrow and silence.

His body shifted uncomfortably, before he said, "Well, uh, maybe not smarter but just as smart. All right... I'll listen. But I don't want to hear it now."

"Why does it take cancer to get you girls out here?" he asked.

"Dad, you know perfectly well we chose a different life-style than you and Eileen. We chose not to raise our family around your drugs. And to be perfectly honest, you gave us up for all of that." I said.

"Ha... you always were my kid with balls." Suddenly without pretense a wave of tenderness washed over my father's face. "You know I love you girls - always have and always will."

Waves of emotion covered us. My sister's tears rolled swiftly down her cheeks. "We love you, too," she said.

"That's why we're here - because we do care," I said.

Our conversation turned to happy memories of family while he lived at home with our mother. We caught Dad up with the news of marriages, children, and his grandchildren's activities.

My father told us the stories of life in the woods of Vermont. "I built our house pretty much myself. I could have done a better job but it's finished now. You'll appreciate the wildlife in Vermont. Hey, by the way, are you staying at my house tonight?"

"Yep! We sure are," Keitly said with feigned joy. I cringed at the thought.

Before he could go on, I said, "We'll stay one night. And Dad, can I pray for your operation before we leave?"

Irritation flashed in his eyes. "All right, Nikki. But make it short." He then laid his head back onto the starched pillow with closed eyes.

"Father, I thank you for my dad. I ask that you guide the doctor with wisdom in tonight's surgery. I pray Lord that you will meet him on that operating table tonight, as it is his hour of need. Please make yourself known to him, in Jesus name, amen."

"Where did she learn to do that?" he asked Keitly.

With a laugh, I leaned over and planted a kiss on his forehead. "We'll check in on you tomorrow."

Our 30-minute drive to our father's house had turned interesting as we came upon a narrow dirt road that snaked a mile through a thick wooded region.

We saw ahead of us, his house standing sloppily at the bottom of a mini-mountain. A small pond sat to the right of the house with heaps of metal trash peaking through a layer of pond scum. Bald tires and a single mattress littered the front yard. "Welcome home," I sighed. "Don't you feel like we just arrived at Ma and Pa Kettle's house in a place called 'no where land'?"

Keitly laughed and said, "Wait till we get inside."

Eileen's "good housekeeping skills" were notoriously absent. So whatever we were about to find inside would only add to our experience.

When we entered the kitchen, we looked to our right and saw a long wooden table placed near several front windows. This table was littered with newspapers and we knew it had offered many a drink and/or drug with conversation centered on their favorite subject, "the world's system and all that's wrong with it."

The sun's beams glistened on the snow-capped trees while on the ground below reflected a junkyard. These windows opened my eyes to God's beauty of creation versus man's sinful destruction. Dad's life could have been beautiful but he spent his gifts and talents on garbage.

"Dad said he saw a bull-moose right in front of the house a week ago. That's an animal I don't want to run into," Keitly said.

"A moose, are you kidding? I pray we don't run into demons. Can you imagine how many live here? All the drug traffic in and out of this house can only be a magnet to all unclean spirits."

"That's enough Nikki. You're scaring me."

"I don't want to scare you but this is the way it is in a home without Christ."

"Hey let's get something to eat," Keit said while scouring the cupboards. "Looks like there's nothing here but a jar of peanut butter; check the fridge for any kind of jelly." After we ate a sandwich, we did the piles of dishes left out in the sink. Keit wiped down the table and I scrubbed the greasy countertops. I looked for a broom but found none. "How do they live without a broom?" I asked.

"Oh forget it, let's go to bed. Eileen is probably at the hospital for the night and I'm exhausted from the 12-hour drive. Besides, I really don't want to be up when their friends arrive," said Keitly.

"Amen," I said. I folded my coat under my head and pulled the blanket to my chin. "Geez, why didn't I think of that? I don't want to see any of their friends tonight."

Our sleep was fitful. The air in the room was heavy and dark. "I suppose this will be a long night," I said. We tossed and turned, laughed and fussed at one another before we fell asleep.

Finally, early morning arrived and we crept out of the house careful not to wake the others in the house. Once outside, we ran for the car in fear of confrontation with anyone in the house. "We made it!" Keitly laughed.

A note stuck to the wiper of our truck. Our half-brother always had a way of reminding us of the unwanted flesh-connection. "Please see me before you leave Vermont." We groaned. "I guess he knew he would miss us this morning," Keit said.

As I drove, I felt swaddled in guilt. I looked over at my sister and asked, "Why did God give us this group of people to be our family?"

With a sigh I stared ahead at the road. "You just never know what life will bring. Do you remember anything about our home in Connecticut?"

"A tiny bit; I remember we had a huge fenced in back-yard," Keitly said.

Yes, Dad worked hard. Besides building a seven-foot fence around an acre of land, he built us a house. Nothing like the one we just left.

"Were you embarrassed Nikki when he was arrested?" Keitly asked.

"No. I was sick. You were just a baby really when all that happened. "Fresh hurt washed over me, because of dad and his drunkenness, I lost my father, friends and home.

"Lord, give me grace. Help me to forgive him – again." I think what was more disappointing is once he had gone to prison for manslaughter, I was positive that he'd do what was right. But I was wrong. He totally went to the opposite end of respectability once he married Eileen. The two with their intellectual trash dug themselves into a deeper hole.

"We all tried to have a relationship with him, and he with us," Keitly said. "You've got to feel sorry for him. He couldn't face himself."

"I guess. But the man ruined his life," I said.

Once we were out in the fresh air of God's winter, we felt the tension release from our bodies. Vermont is beautiful in winter. East Corinth, the nearest town to dad's house, had a 'Walton's Mountain' feel to it. The main street had a general store with old-fashioned gas pumps that stood side by side. A small white post office with a red door neighbored the store by a little less than a city block. Further down the road we came to a diner called 'The Little Brown Bear' where we had pancakes with Vermont's famous hot maple syrup.

We rented a cheap clean motel room, a few miles away from dad's house, and then we headed for the hospital.

"He's still in recovery," a nurse said. Her broad face showed no compassion as she pushed a strand of red hair back from her face.

"What's the prognosis? Do you know?" I asked her.

"It's not for me to say, the doctor will be in later today," she turned her back to us.

"He's dying, Keit – we need to stay until he wakes up."

"Nikki, let's just go back to the room, he'll be out of it for hours." she said. We drove back to the motel, questions bombarded my mind. Dad's dying, and Keitly didn't want me to share Jesus with him? My other two sisters who aren't Christians didn't even want to ride with me or be on the same trip. 'Lord, I get tired of being the only one in the family that speaks out. Why doesn't Keitly go to church? She has bumper stickers all over the back of her car about you, but shrinks back in front of family whenever your name is mentioned. Why? Why am I so offended by her embarrassment?'

That night Devon came to visit us at our motel room. My half-brother's height and build reminded me of the pictures of Dad when he was young. He wore a blue logger's shirt with jeans and construction boots. "I didn't want my sisters to leave without us getting to know one another a little better," he said.

"I missed having you around while I was growing up," Devon said.

"It's a bit hard to have a relationship with a brother that is at least two decades younger than we are," I said. "I don't say this to hurt you but how can we know our brothers as we are not only miles but ages apart plus a drug life-style that separates us?"

Devon looked down at the floor and said, "They don't sell marijuana anymore."

"Good," Keitly said. "Did they stop selling cocaine?"

"They stopped dealing all drugs," he said.

"No offense, but we've heard that before. Too many times before," I said. "How has it been for you? I mean, do you do drugs too?"

"No, er, I did some drugs but stopped when they stopped." His large dark eyes looked at us. "I don't know what you think of this, but I do drink."

"It's not wrong to drink but it is a sin to get drunk," I said.

Keitly blushed and rolled her eyes. She laid her back against the wall with her legs crossed Indian style.

"Devon, I want you to know that there is someone who loves and does accept you," I said.

Keitly's legs uncurled and she got up to sit on the edge of the bed.

I went on with "Jesus will help you. He will give you hope and a future."

"I don't believe that there is a god. Or he wouldn't let bad things happen in this world. Did he love Hitler too? Come on, Nikki. Bible stories are simply that, stories," Devon said.

"Now you sound just like dad. Have you read any part of the Bible?" I asked. I watched my sister from the corner of my eye get up and pull her jeans out of her suitcase. "Why don't you read the gospel of John so you can debate your beliefs intelligently?"

"Hey Devon, let's go for a beer or a cup of coffee," said Keitly.

"It's so late. I'm in my pajamas," I said.

"You don't have to come. I'm sure you're exhausted. Devon and I will go out for an hour or so."

A slow burn stirred in my chest.

"Don't wait up for me. I'll see you in the morning."

Once they shut the door, I fell into my pillow and wept. "Lord, please help Keitly and me to stand together without division. Help her not to shun me."

I slept fitfully throughout the night. I could hear the voices from the past declare, "I don't want what you have. Life isn't all about Jesus; what's happened to you?" I heard the voices of my husband, sisters, mother and old friends. I remembered the pain when those voices went silent. No more phone calls or family invitations to get together. Neighbors laughed at me and declared me to be out of my mind. Even the black sheep of the family, my dad, avoided and ridiculed me to the rest of the family.

When the morning rays shone through the cheap curtains of our motel room, I rose up from my bed and headed to the shower.

"Nikki – guess what!" I turned around to see Keitly in bed with a huge smile upon her face.

"I don't have a clue," I said with an edge in my voice. "Did you and Devon stay out all night?"

"No way. But we did go to the hospital after a beer. Dad was awake and the first thing he said to me was, "I saw Jesus and it wasn't good.""

My sister's eyes were almost as wide as her smile. "He answered your prayer."

I sat on her bed and said, "What did he say about Jesus?"

"He didn't elaborate. He was agitated though."

"Sis, I know you love the Lord, but why do you get embarrassed with my sharing Jesus?" I asked.

With downcast eyes Keitly said, "Look, when I took Devon out for a drink he said he now sees why dad mocks you."

"I told him that you are absolutely right and dad is wrong about Christ and the Bible. I told him that everything you said was true. I guess I'm a person that wants peace at any cost. I know that is wrong. I'm still a work in process.

"I am too. I can come off too strong. Sorry if I embarrass you," I said. "But on the other hand, dad is on the edge of spending an eternity in hell. There is no time. I've got to share with him, and with his family and friends, while we are here. Are you with me?"

"I'm with you, Nikki. I'll follow your lead."

That afternoon we walked into dad's hospital room. I noticed the physician, nurses and several other people in the room. As we approached his bed, my father yelled out, "Hey there! Take a good look at these beauties – I'll let you have them for fifty bucks a night."

My hands waved for him to be quiet. I saw the glances between the medical staff.

Dad's voice rose in mocking laughter, "Oh dad, please don't."

I looked at the physician and asked him if I could talk with him in the hall. "Can you please tell me the results and prognosis of my father's condition?"

"Take your filthy hands off of me you b......," my dad shouted at a male nurse.

"Your father's lung cancer has spread to his brain," he said. "If you're wondering how long he's got, I can't tell you exactly. I give him a few weeks."

"My family and I thank you for all that you have done for him." The doctor nodded and looked at me with sympathy.

The next morning we visited my dad in a private room where he lay weak and pale. Eileen with three of her four children sat near his bed. Their sons and friends too were visiting.

I waited for the opportunity that God would give to me to speak. My step-sister Alyssa asked me, "Please tell us what has happened to you with God." It was then I shared the entire gospel of Jesus Christ with the whole room and gave testimony to his great love and desire for each to call unto Him for salvation with confession of sin and repentance. I reminded my stepmother, stepsiblings, and their friends of what a messed up, suicidal, raging young woman I had been. Surely they could attest to the dramatic difference that Jesus has made in my life. Silence fell throughout the room once I had finished. Then Keitly quietly sang the song Amazing Grace.

We left the hospital that day in peace.

Once I arrived home I told Stephanie about the entire visit. "Mom, I'm going to pray that God will show grandpa what's waiting for him after he dies – hell." I heard the exasperation and conviction in her voice. The hair on my arms rose.

Every couple of days I called my dad on the phone just to talk. I never brought up the gospel in these conversations. I just loved him. He lived for another two months.

Ten days before he died, I called him and asked him the usual, "How are you feeling today?"

"Terrible. Awful."

"Oh dad, are you in pain?" I asked.

"No, it isn't that. It's every time I fall asleep, I see myself being pulled down into this black pit by huge demons. And what bothers me most, Nikki, is that I am pulling a whole lot of people down with me."

My heart began to beat a little faster with a tremor in my voice I said, "Stephanie, prayed that you would see where you will spend eternity without Christ. Dad, these things are real. Demons, angels, hell and heaven are real. Jesus Christ is the only way out of hell. Call out to him. Confess your sins and ask him for forgiveness. He loves you, and I promise he will forgive you. But you must believe that He took your punishment on that cross and rose from the dead three days later. He is the resurrection and the life."

My father listened. He promised me he'd do what I asked him to do. Days later I called my dad and he spoke to me in a voice with high excitement yet his speech was garbled and I couldn't understand one word.

Dad died the following day while I was on the phone with his son, my brother, Devon. We wept and grieved together as a family that hour.

Later that night, I heard the voice of doubt. "Did he really ask Christ to forgive and save him? Was his confession real?"

The phone rang and it was Jody, "Nikki, I wanted to tell you how proud of you I am. We may not see eye to eye on religion but I know dad is in heaven. I couldn't believe the difference I heard in his voice. He no longer cursed or made fun of you anymore. Do you think it had anything to with the medication he was on?"

"No, Jody. It is because he met Jesus Christ, and dad now is in heaven."

I rejoice in the work of Jesus. I wait in expectation for His continued work in my family and I stand in awe of His extra ordinary work in one ordinary life.

CPSIA information can be obtained
at www.ICGtesting.com
Printed in the USA
FSOW03n0856131117
41107FS